Rely on Thomas Cook as your travelling companion on your next trip and benefit from our unique heritage.

Thomas Cook **pocket** guides

SARDINIA

Your travelling companion since 1873

Written and updated by Marc Di Duca

Published by Thomas Cook Publishing
A division of Thomas Cook Tour Operations Limited
Company registration no. 3772199 England
The Thomas Cook Business Park, Unit 9, Coningsby Road,
Peterborough PE3 8SB, United Kingdom
Email: books@thomascook.com, Tel: + 44 (0) 1733 416 477
www.thomascookpublishing.com

Produced by Cambridge Publishing Management Limited
Burr Elm Court, Main Street, Caldecote CB23 7NU

ISBN: 978-1-84848-265-4

First edition © 2008 Thomas Cook Publishing
This second edition © 2010
Text © Thomas Cook Publishing
Maps © Thomas Cook Publishing/PCGraphics (UK) Limited

Series Editor: Adam Royal
Production/DTP: Steven Collins

Printed and bound in Spain by GraphyCems

Cover photography © Jan Richter, Photolibrary

All rights reserved. No part of this publication may be reproduced, stored in a retrieval system or transmitted, in any form or by any means, electronic, mechanical, recording or otherwise, in any part of the world, without prior permission of the publisher. Requests for permission should be made to the publisher at the above address.

Although every care has been taken in compiling this publication, and the contents are believed to be correct at the time of printing, Thomas Cook Tour Operations Limited cannot accept any responsibility for errors or omissions, however caused, or for changes in details given in the guidebook, or for the consequences of any reliance on the information provided. Descriptions and assessments are based on the author's views and experiences when writing and do not necessarily represent those of Thomas Cook Tour Operations Limited.

CONTENTS

INTRODUCTION 5
Getting to know Sardinia 8
The best of Sardinia 10
Symbols key 12

RESORTS 13
Cagliari 15
Pula & Nora 25
Bosa 31
Alghero 37
Stintino 47
Castelsardo 51
Porto Cervo 55
Villasimius 59

EXCURSIONS 63
Sassari 64
Oristano 69
Iglesias 73
Nuraghe Santu Antine 77
La Maddalena Archipelago 80

LIFESTYLE 85
Food & drink 86
Menu decoder 90
Shopping 93
Children 96
Sports & activities 98
Festivals & events 100

PRACTICAL INFORMATION 103
Accommodation 104
Preparing to go 106
During your stay 114

INDEX 125

MAPS
Sardinia 6
Cagliari 14
Pula 26
Bosa 32
Alghero 38
Castelsardo 50
Villasimius 58

POCKET GUIDES

> **WHAT'S IN YOUR GUIDEBOOK?**
>
> **Independent authors** Impartial, up-to-date information from our travel experts who meticulously source local knowledge.
>
> **Experience** Thomas Cook's 165 years in the travel industry and guidebook publishing enriches every word with expertise you can trust.
>
> **Travel know-how** Thomas Cook has thousands of staff working around the globe, all living and breathing travel.
>
> **Editors** Travel-publishing professionals, pulling everything together to craft a perfect blend of words, pictures, maps and design.
>
> **You, the traveller** We deliver a practical, no-nonsense approach to information, geared to how you really use it.

ABOUT THE AUTHOR

Marc Di Duca is an established travel guide author with numerous titles to his name, including guides to destinations as diverse as Madeira, Prague and Siberia. He has written and updated dozens of books for leading travel publishers such as Thomas Cook, Bradt, Lonely Planet and Cicerone, and freelances for a number of websites and travel magazines in Europe.

▶ *View of Cagliari, the capital of Sardinia*

INTRODUCTION
Getting to know Sardinia

INTRODUCTION

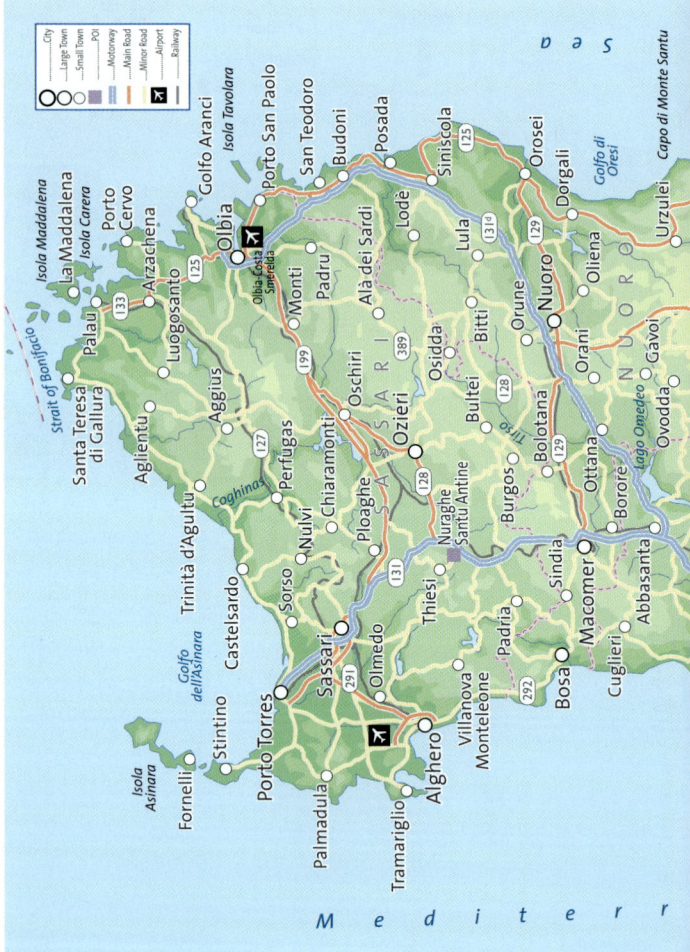

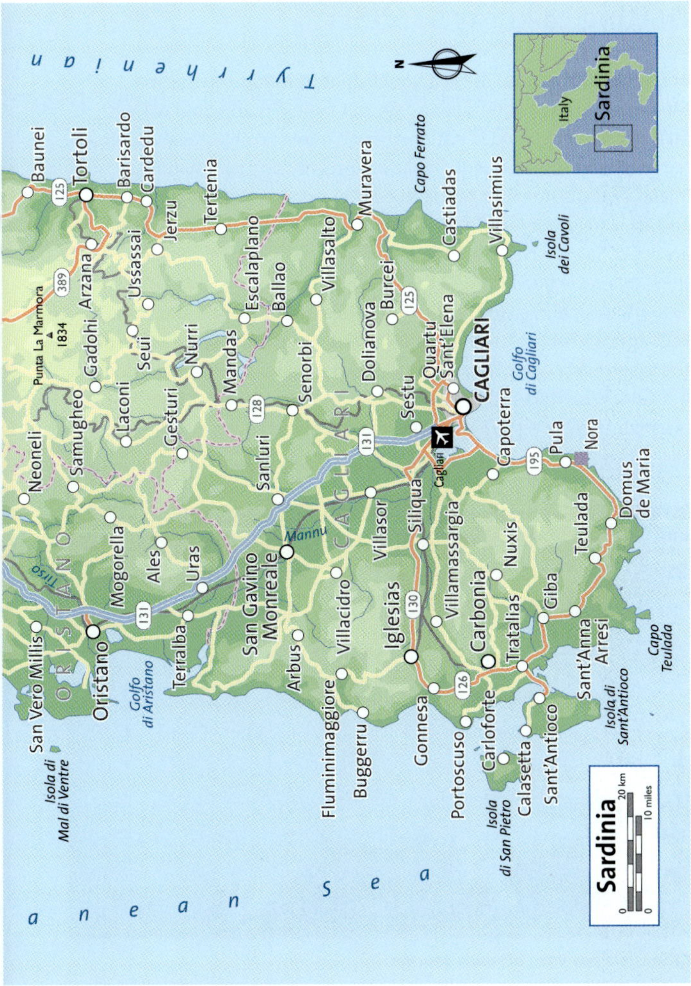
Sardinia
0 20 km
0 10 miles
Italy
Sardinia
N
Tyrrhenian Sea
CAGLIARI
Cagliari
Oristano
Iglesias
Carbonia
Tortolì
San Gavino Monreale
ORISTANO
CAGLIARI
Baunei
Barisardo
Cardedu
Tertenia
Jerzu
Ussassai
Arzana
Gadoni
Punta La Marmora
1834
Seui
Nurri
Laconi
Samugheo
Neoneli
Gesturi
Mandas
Escalaplano
Ballao
Villasalto
Muravera
Burcei
Dolianova
Senorbì
Sanluri
Sestu
Quartu Sant'Elena
Castiadas
Villasimius
Capo Ferrato
Isola dei Cavoli
Golfo di Cagliari
Capoterra
Pula
Nora
Domus de Maria
Teulada
Capo Teulada
Nuxis
Giba
Sant'Anna Arresi
Tratalias
Villamassargia
Siliqua
Villasor
Villacidro
Mannu
Arbus
Fluminimaggiore
Buggerru
Gonnesa
Portoscuso
Carloforte
Isola di San Pietro
Calasetta
Sant'Antioco
Isola di Sant'Antioco
Terralba
Uras
Ales
Mogorella
Tirso
San Vero Milis
Isola di Mal di Ventre
Golfo di Aristano
125
389
128
131
130
126
195

INTRODUCTION

Getting to know Sardinia

At the heart of a turquoise sea, equidistant from Tunis, Rome and Monaco, lies the Mediterranean's second-largest island, Sardinia, with an independently minded nation, though unmistakably Italian. Geology has given this island miles of exquisite beaches and commanding inland peaks, history has bequeathed over 5,000 years of architecture and art, and invaders from the Carthaginians of North Africa to the armies of Savoy have all left their mark on Sardinia's cities and in the locals' gene pool.

Sardinia is also a land of tradition where colourful arts and crafts are kept alive and at least one religious festival takes place somewhere on the island every week. All of this, plus some superb local food and long, hot summers, makes Sardinia one of the Mediterranean's most fascinating, relaxing and enjoyable holiday destinations.

● *Sardinia has miles of sandy beaches*

Relatively undiscovered and certainly not a mass-market, high-rise destination, Sardinia retains a low-key atmosphere in many places. That said, the island's beaches are some of the best in Italy and an adequate tourist infrastructure around the coast caters for holidaymakers' every need. Venture inland a short distance and you will discover a remote, unspoilt traditional interior with rugged mountain terrain and wide plains dotted with prehistoric sites built by the mysterious Nuraghic peoples, as well as large towns such as Sassari, Oristano and Nuoro.

This contrast between the coastal holiday resorts and Sardinia's hinterland of shepherds, tradition and historical legacy gives Sardinia an added dimension, making a holiday there so much more than just turning bronze on the beach.

Sardinia has become much simpler to reach in recent years thanks to flights operated by budget airlines (see page 106), though many still choose the more traditional way of travelling – namely ferry from mainland Italy and France. However you arrive and wherever you holiday on the island, Sardinia will never disappoint.

D H LAWRENCE IN SARDINIA

The only work of English literature on Sardinia is a curious little travelogue called *Sea and Sardinia* written by author D H Lawrence in the 1920s, following a whirlwind off-season trip from Cagliari to the ferry port at Olbia via the mountains. Apart from becoming increasingly irate at conditions he and q-b (Queen Bee, his German wife) encounter in various inns and guesthouses, and berating fellow travellers for their views on the exchange rate between the pound and the lira, Lawrence provides a snapshot of life on the island 80 years ago. However, his descriptions of rotten food, stinking accommodation and the biting cold do little to promote Sardinia as a tourist destination!

THE BEST OF SARDINIA

Sardinia is brimming with countless great places to go and things to see and do. From Cagliari's historic centre to the rural backdrop of the prehistoric Nuraghe, from the informal family atmosphere of Alghero to the exclusivity of the Costa Smeralda resorts, this sunny island truly has something for everybody to enjoy.

TOP 10 ATTRACTIONS

- **Stunning beaches and turquoise seas** The reason most people come to Sardinia. And if you thought the photos in the holiday brochure weren't entirely genuine, the deep emeralds and turquoises of the water contrasting with the white sands ashore are sure to change your mind (see pages 15 and 25).

- **A ride on the narrow-gauge *trenino verde* (little green train) through the island's dramatic interior** The best way to see the spectacular rocky interior without getting blisters (see page 33).

- **Cagliari, the island's bustling capital** Stroll the boulevards, visit a museum, enjoy a little light lunch, indulge in a bout of retail therapy, and end the day with a glass of wine and a plate of seafood – only in the capital (see page 15).

- **Castelsardo's old town** Explore the enchanting old town of this picturesque north coast resort (see page 51).

- **Neptune's Grotto near Alghero** The most entertaining way to get out of the sun and cool down on the north coast (see page 43).

- **Religious festivals and celebrations** Sardinians will use any excuse to party and have done for centuries. Even D H Lawrence found that being around for one of these shindigs added a bit of colour to his holiday (see page 100).

- **Sardinia's Nuraghic sites** Older than Stonehenge and still no one knows exactly what they were for. Why not enjoy a spot of Nuraghe-spotting on long train or car journeys with the kids (see page 77)?

- **The ancient ruins at Nora and Tharros** Clamber among the fallen columns and deserted amphitheatres of Sardinia's once great Roman ports (see pages 27 and 70).

- **The exclusive resorts and beaches of the Costa Smeralda** Rub shoulders with Italy's rich and famous at some of the Med's most expensive and exclusive resorts (see page 55).

- **Tucking into a plate of delicious Sardinian seafood** And it's not all sardines (see page 86)!

◐ *A tranquil port near La Maddalena (see pages 80–4)*

INTRODUCTION

SYMBOLS KEY
The following symbols are used throughout this book:

❸ address ❶ telephone ⓦ website address ❸ email
❶ opening times ❸ how to get there ❶ important

The following symbols are used on the maps:

- 🛈 information office
- 🛍 shopping
- ✈ airport
- ✚ hospital
- 🚌 bus station
- ✝ church
- — railway
- ❶ numbers denote featured cafés, restaurants & evening venues
- ○ city
- ○ large town
- ○ small town
- ■ POI (point of interest)
- ═ motorway
- — main road
- — minor road

RESTAURANT CATEGORIES
The symbol after the name of each restaurant listed in this guide indicates the price of a typical main course plus starter or dessert and drink for one person.
£ under €15   ££ €15–€30   £££ over €30

▶ *Cagliari from Bastione San Remy*

RESORTS
Places under the sun

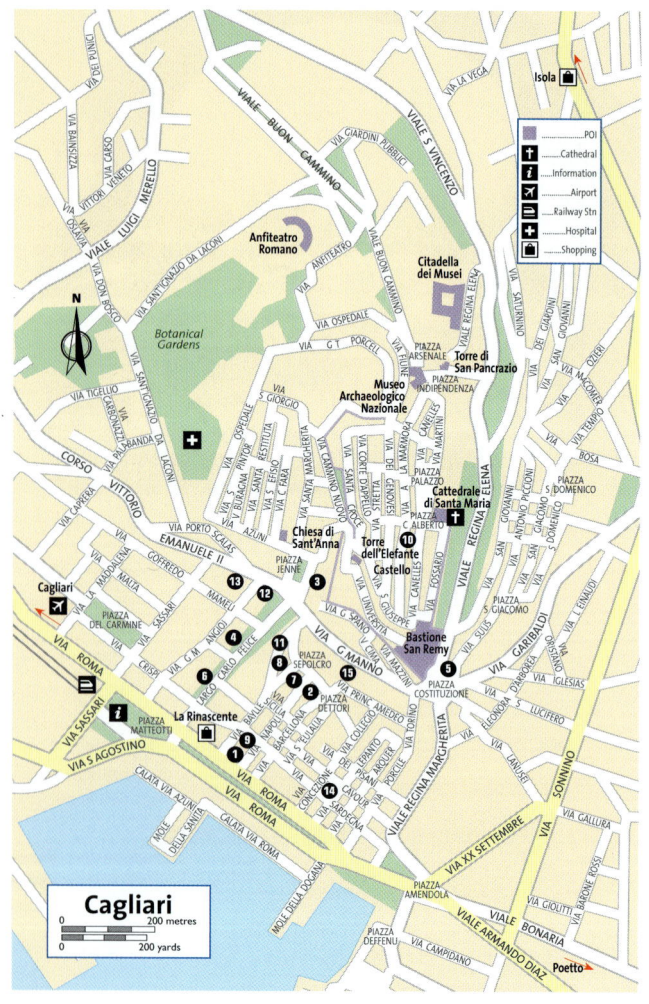

Cagliari

By far Sardinia's largest city and the capital since Roman times, Cagliari is the focal point of the Sardinian world. No visit to the island can be deemed complete without a stroll around its tightly packed medieval centre, a climb up to the Castello or a night on the tiles at some of the best bars on the island. The city's many museums, galleries, churches and other attractions are all set against a stunning backdrop of imposing mountain peaks, while the sea shimmers beyond the port. There's even a fine white-sand beach at nearby Poetto, a short bus ride away.

The centre of Cagliari is divided into distinct neighbourhoods. The **Marina** is the knot of narrow medieval streets just back from the seafront where you will discover some of the best restaurants and shops. The **Stampace**, to the north, holds much of the city's historic heritage with churches and a Roman amphitheatre vying for the visitor's attention. **Villanova** represents Cagliari's 19th-century extension, while the highlight of the centre must be the **Castello** with its cathedral, imposing palaces and historic narrow lanes where tall town houses rising four or five storeys are still inhabited by the city's poor.

Cagliari is one of Sardinia's more tourist-friendly spots and English-speakers are well catered for with signs in English gracing most tourist sights. Even the standard of English in most eateries and at tourist sights is better than in other resorts (except Alghero).

New development in Cagliari includes a tram system, which is as yet not fully operational. Also in progress is the Mediterranean Museum of Nuraghic and Contemporary Art. At time of writing still a building site on the sea front, this major new museum project is set to become one of the island's main tourist attractions in years to come. Designed by the world-famous British-Iraqi architect Zaha Hadid, the futuristic structure will provide an impressive roof beneath which all of Sardinia's Nuraghic heritage can be gathered.

RESORTS

BEACHES

Poetto, situated 5 km (3 miles) east of the city centre, is the nearest stretch of real beach to Cagliari (forget the pitiful few grains of sand at Calamosca). Few fail to be impressed by the bleached sand shelving gently into the glittering emerald waters of the Med set against a backdrop of a high bluff of land called the **Sella del Diavolo (Devil's Saddle)**, thanks to its shape, which divides Poetto from Cagliari. It's a great bit of beach, but unfortunately on hot days most of Cagliari's inhabitants think the same and descend on Poetta in their thousands. The overcrowding is compounded by most of the beach being cordoned off and used as private sunbathing areas for hotels lining the shore.

❶ To reach Poetto take bus PF or PQ from Piazza Matteotti. The journey takes around 15 minutes.

🔺 *Sella del Diavolo*

THINGS TO SEE & DO

Anfiteatro Romano (Roman Amphitheatre)
Hewn out of solid rock, Cagliari's huge amphitheatre is one of the most impressive sights in the city. Though much of the stone was carted off in the Middle Ages as building material, large stretches of the original arena survive. Open-air performances still take place here in summer (though minus the Christians and lions).

ⓐ Via Anfiteatro ⓣ 070 65 29 56 ⓦ www.anfiteatroromano.it
🕘 09.30–13.30 Tues–Sat, 09.30–13.30, 15.30–17.30 Sun (Apr–Oct); 09.30–13.30 Tues–Sat, 10.00–13.00 Sun (Nov–Mar)
❗ Admission charge

Bastione San Remy (Bastion of St Remy)
Many access the Castello from **Piazza Costituzione** by climbing the steps of the grand Bastione San Remy on the southern flank dating from the early 20th century. Seen from above, the steps emerge through a huge hole in the ramparts, not at all obvious when you are there. The stupendous views from the top are worth the climb.

ⓐ Castello

Castello (Castle)
On a hilltop high above the town and port below rises Cagliari's huge Castello, more of an area of town than a castle, though its boundaries are marked by high, beefy ramparts. Since medieval times it has been the traditional seat of power of the government and the Church in Sardinia, hence the spectacular architecture dating from various periods. In addition to the specific places of interest it contains, the Castello is also riddled with narrow, dark and very atmospheric alleyways where washing is draped between wrought-iron balconies, the aroma of cooking hangs in the air and where little has changed in centuries. This is the only part of Cagliari where you can still see World War II bomb damage with many conspicuous rubble-filled gaps in several streets.

❗ Admission charge

RESORTS

Cattedrale di Santa Maria (Cathedral of St Mary)
Perhaps the most impressive building within the Castello complex is the cathedral, situated in Piazza Palazzo – the historic area of the Castello. The building's recently sand-blasted Tuscan-Romanesque façade decorated with rows of blind arches and Byzantine-style icons hides a Gothic and baroque interior packed with precious works of art and sporting a glorious painted ceiling. Visitors can also descend into the crypt, which contains tombs belonging to various royal and noble families. Next door to the cathedral extends the grand symmetrical façade of the **Palazzo Viceregio**.
ⓐ Piazza Palazzo 4 ⓣ 070 66 38 37 ⓛ 08.00–12.30, 16.00–19.00 Mon–Sat, 08.00–13.00, 16.00–20.00 Sun

Chiesa di Sant'Anna (Church of St Anne)
Cagliari has many churches but possibly the grandest is the Church of St Anne in the Stampace quarter, a neoclassical edifice which rises confidently at the top of a sweeping flight of stone steps. It took almost 150 years to complete and no sooner had work finished in the 1930s than the building took a direct hit from a World War II bomb in 1943. The late baroque interior has been painstakingly restored.
ⓐ Via Azuni ⓛ 08.00–13.00 & 15.30–20.00

Cittadella dei Musei (Museum Citadel)
Just off Piazza dell'Arsenale at the northern end of the Castello you will find a fascinating complex of four museums which could easily occupy an entire day. The two heavyweights of the quartet are the **Museo Archeologico Nazionale (National Archaeological Museum)**, which houses collections dating from the Stone Age to Roman times, and the **Pinoteca Nazionale (National Art Museum)**, whose collection of works dating from the 15th to 17th centuries (with a floor of late 19th- and early 20th-century works thrown in for good measure) is second to none on the island. The **Museo d'Arte Siamese (Siamese Art Museum)** represents the passion of one Stefano Cardu for all things Thai. Over 20 years he collected a vast amount of art from Thailand and Southeast Asia while

CAGLIARI

◐ *The amphitheatre in Cagliari is magnificent*

RESORTS

> **SHOPPING**
> **ISOLA** The Cagliari branch of ISOLA is situated to the north of the city centre and stocks a wide range of ceramics, jewellery, basketware, carpets, tapestries, traditional knives and furniture.
> ⓐ Via Bacaredda 176 ⓣ 070 49 27 56 ⓛ 09.00–13.00 & 15.00–19.00 ⓜ Bus M from Piazza Matteotti
> **La Rinascente** This large department store is one of 14 across Italy and the biggest in Sardinia. Italy's answer to the UK-wide department store John Lewis and stocks almost anything you could think of. However, prices are inflated and Italian baroque-style luxury may not exactly be to Anglo Saxon tastes.
> ⓐ Via Roma 109 ⓣ 070 60 451 ⓦ www.rinascente.it ⓛ 09.00–20.30

working as an engineer in the region. Unless you have a specific interest in anatomy, leave the **Collezione di Cere Anatomiche (Collection of Anatomical Waxworks)**, 23 gory studies in wax and resin by the Florentine sculptor Clemente Susini, until last.

Museum Citadel ⓣ 070 67 57 627 ⓛ 08.30–20.00
National Archaeological Museum ⓛ 09.00–14.00, 15.00–20.00 Tues–Sun (Apr–Sept); 09.00–19.00 Tues–Sun (Oct–Mar) ⓘ Admission charge except under-18s and over-60s
National Art Museum ⓣ 070 67 40 54 ⓛ 08.30–19.00 ⓘ Admission charge except under-18s and over-60s
Siamese Art Museum ⓣ 070 65 18 88 ⓛ 09.00–13.00, 15.30–19.30 Tues–Sun ⓘ Admission charge except under-5s, over-60s and visitors with disabilities
Collection of Anatomical Waxworks ⓣ 070 67 57 627 ⓛ 09.00–13.00 & 16.00–19.00

Orto Botanico (Botanical Gardens)
The greenery of Cagliari's botanical gardens comes as something of a relief after all that sun-bleached limestone. Moved to this site in the late

19th century, the lush gardens contain 500 species of plant and are some of the best in Italy.
ⓐ Via Sant'Ignazio da Laconi ⓣ 070 67 53 522 ⓛ 08.00–13.30, 15.00–19.00

Torre dell'Elefante (Elephant Tower)
Another access point into the Castello is from **Piazza Yenne**, climbing the flight of steps in the far northern corner of the square or taking the lift. Whichever way you choose, you will end up at the four-storey Pisan, white limetone **Torre dell'Elefante**, a defensive tower built in 1307, which can be climbed for even better panoramic views across the city and beyond. This tower and the **Torre di San Pancrazio** (see below) seem strangely unfinished as their back walls are missing. This could have been a clever design allowing easier access in times of attack or just a money-saving exercise on the Pisans' part.
ⓐ Via Università, Historic Centre, Cagliari ⓛ 09.00–17.00

Torre di San Pancrazio (St Pancras' Tower)
The northern reaches of the Castello were protected by another tall 13th-century white limestone Pisan tower, the Torre di San Pancrazio, which can also be scaled for an almost bird's-eye view of the bustling Sardinian capital.
ⓐ Piazza Indipendenza e Via Università ⓛ 09.00–13.00, 16.00–19.30 Tues–Sun (Apr–Oct); 09.00–16.30 Tues–Sun (Nov–Mar)

EXCURSION
CTM OPEN Trambus In a city of Cagliari's size and hilliness the open-top bus tours run by the city transport company CTM are a welcome addition for tourists. For just 10 euros you can hop on and off as much as you like and tickets (available on the bus) are valid for the whole day. If you just sit on board and look at the sights from the comfort of the sleek, modern, pillar-box red buses, the tour takes about an hour and is narrated in English, Italian and French. The best place to board is Piazza Yenne. Tours last one hour.
ⓛ 10.00, 11.00, 12.00, 13.00, 16.00, 17.00, 18.00, 19.00 (mid-Apr–June & last

RESORTS

half of Sept); 10.00, 10.30, 11.00, 11.30, 12.00, 12.30, 13.00, 16.00, 16.30, 17.00, 17.30, 18.00, 18.30, 19.00, 19.30 (July–mid-Sept)
❶ Admission charge except children under 4 years

TAKING A BREAK

Café Roma £ ❶ This is one of the best places that shelter under the arcading on lively Via Roma. The location creates the perfect setting to watch the world squeeze its way between the tables or race past on two and four wheels. Write your postcards here while slurping a frothy cappuccino served by very well turned-out waiters. ⓐ Via Roma 109 ⓑ 05.00–24.00

Caffè Barcellona £ ❷ Located in the tightly packed streets of the Marina district, the Barcellona has been delighting coffee-bean aficionados for 50 years, though from the modern décor you would never guess. ⓐ Via Barcellona 84 ⓣ 070 65 97 12 ⓑ 07.30–21.30 Mon–Sat

Isola Del Gelato £ ❸ The 'Ice Cream Island' is a popular *gelateria* and one of the best places in town to grab a scoop or two from the myriad flavours. The shop is like a cave full of ice cream and is kept at a very low temperature even when it's pushing 40 degrees outside. ⓐ Piazza Jenne 35 ⓣ 070 65 98 24 ⓑ 09.00–late

The Living Room £ ❹ The extra-strong air-con at this hip and trendy bar-cum-café with its beige décor and wavy bar means you can chill here in more ways than one. ⓐ Largo Carlo Felice 52 ⓣ 070 65 03 32 ⓑ 07.00–02.00 Mon–Sat

Antico Caffè £–££ ❺ Treat yourself to a bit of old world charm at this Cagliari institution in the shadow of the Bastione Remy. The local pasta and seafood combinations, crêpes, salads and 50 types of cocktail, plus the charmingly old-fashioned dining room with its scurrying uniformed waiters and ceiling fans, make you feel you could spend all day here watching the world race across Piazza Costituzione. ⓐ Piazza Costituzione 10/11 ❶ 070 65 82 06 🕒 07.00–02.00

Caffè Svizzero £–££ ❻ Possibly Cagliari's best coffee institution with a history going back almost a century. Enjoy a leisurely breakfast of coffee and pastries served by smart waiters in an elegant setting under the high vaulted ceiling. ⓐ Largo Carlo Felice 6 ❶ 070 65 37 84 🕒 07.00–21.00

Antico Galeone ££ ❼ This intimate restaurant has a nautical theme, a buffet at lunchtime, a set menu of the highest quality in the evenings and Scottish and Belgian ales on tap. ⓐ Via Savoia 1 ❶ 070 65 39 83 🕒 12.30–15.00, 20.00–late ❗ There are only seven tables so reservations are advised

Manàmanà ££ ❽ Write postcards over a coffee or munch salad over a book on one of Cagliari's prettiest squares at this laid-back hangout. ⓐ Via Savoia 15 ❶ 070 65 17 59 ⓦ www.manamana.info 🕒 12.00–01.00 Mon–Fri, 18.30–01.30 Sat

Al Porto ££ ❾ For a delectable Sardinian seafood platter, visit this charming place, which is set just back from the seafront. The expertly prepared dishes are enjoyed in a cosy atmosphere. ⓐ Via Sardegna 44 ❶ 070 66 31 31 🕒 closed Mon

AFTER DARK

Restaurants & bars
King George Pub £ ❿ This tavern is the most convincing British pub on the island with dark timber tables, Victorian wallpaper, wooden floors and stained glass. Were it not almost 40 degrees outside you'd think you were in Blighty. Upstairs in the restaurant things get a touch more Italian. The barmaids pull a fine British pint and there's live music at weekends. ⓐ Via Baylle 77/79 ❶ 070 66 04 88 🕒 10.00–15.00, 18.00–02.00 Tues–Sun

RESORTS

TieRre £ ⓫ Revolution is in the air at this small bar hidden in the atmospheric narrow lanes of the Castello. Allegedly run by a cooperative of Sardinian separatists, the interior is lined with portraits of Sardinian bandits and the Latin-American music nights express solidarity with separatist movements around the world. All the meat and fish dishes are made with organic ingredients and the superb wine is supplied by local producers. Possibly not the best place to sport that souvenir AC Milan football strip! ⓐ Via Lamarmora 45 ⓛ 11.00–04.00

4 Mori ££ ⓬ Rub shoulders with your fellow diners at this simple, intimate Cagliari institution where the focus is firmly on food of the highest quality. The name refers to the four Moors on the Sardinian flag. ⓐ Via Angioj 93 ⓣ 070 65 02 69 ⓛ 13.00–14.30, 20.30–23.30; closed Sun night & Mon ⓘ Reservations recommended

Convento di San Francesco ££ ⓭ This wonderful restaurant is situated under the fabulous vaulted ceiling of a former convent. The setting is almost as good as the food, enjoyed at stylishly laid tables, and the non-Italian staff speak good English. ⓐ Corso V Emanuele II 56 ⓣ 070 65 45 70 ⓛ 08.00–02.00

Lillicu ££ ⓮ Well hidden in the backstreets of the Marina district, Lillicu is one of the few places in Sardinia to have a menu in English – you will know what to expect if you order snails, tripe or horse meat. This is another temple to Sardinian cuisine with simple décor, tightly packed benches and a focus firmly on good food prepared with Sardinian passion and the freshest ingredients. ⓐ Via Sardegna 78 ⓣ 070 65 29 70 ⓦ www.lillicu.com ⓛ 13.00–15.00 & 20.30–23.00 Mon–Sat

Su Procciu ££ ⓯ The Cagliaresi have tried to keep this secret by burying it underground like bottles of *filu 'e ferru*. Head down the steps into the Portico San Antonio on Via Manno to discover a trendy cellar dining space and waiters serving guests a fixed menu of locally caught fish. ⓐ Portico S. Antonio 3 ⓣ 070 65 06 43 ⓛ 12.30–15.00, 20.00–late

Pula & Nora

The compact provincial town of Pula, 3 km (2 miles) inland from the Med, has become a favourite stopover for tourists thanks to the nearby archaeological site at Nora, large hotel complexes further along the coast and some wonderful beaches lining the southern shore.

The town boasts several worthwhile eateries and some light sightseeing. The fantastic white beaches are another major attraction, but when not roasting themselves by the sea, visitors can be found exploring the ancient photogenic remains at Nora, wandering Pula's old streets or enjoying a drink and a free concert in the Piazza del Popolo.

BEACHES

Some 3 km (2 miles) to the south of Pula there are two superb sun-bleached sandy beaches. The Spiaggia di Su Guventeddu extends to the north while the Spiaggia di Nora almost reaches the ruins of the Roman port. The sheer beauty of the setting and its proximity to Nora and Pula mean things can get crowded here in the summer months.

THINGS TO SEE & DO

Chiesa di San Giovanni Battista (Church of St John the Baptist)
Often confused with the Church of St Ephisius in Nora, Pula's main place of worship is a pleasing neoclassical affair and worth a few minutes' inspection, if only to escape from the afternoon heat in its cool interior.
ⓐ Near Piazza Giovanni XXIII, Pula

Chiesa di Sant'Efisio (Church of St Ephisius)
This unremarkable church, which stands just a few steps back from the beach, would go wholly unnoticed if it weren't for its role in the island's biggest festival, the **Festa di Sant'Efisio** (see page 101). Every 1 May,

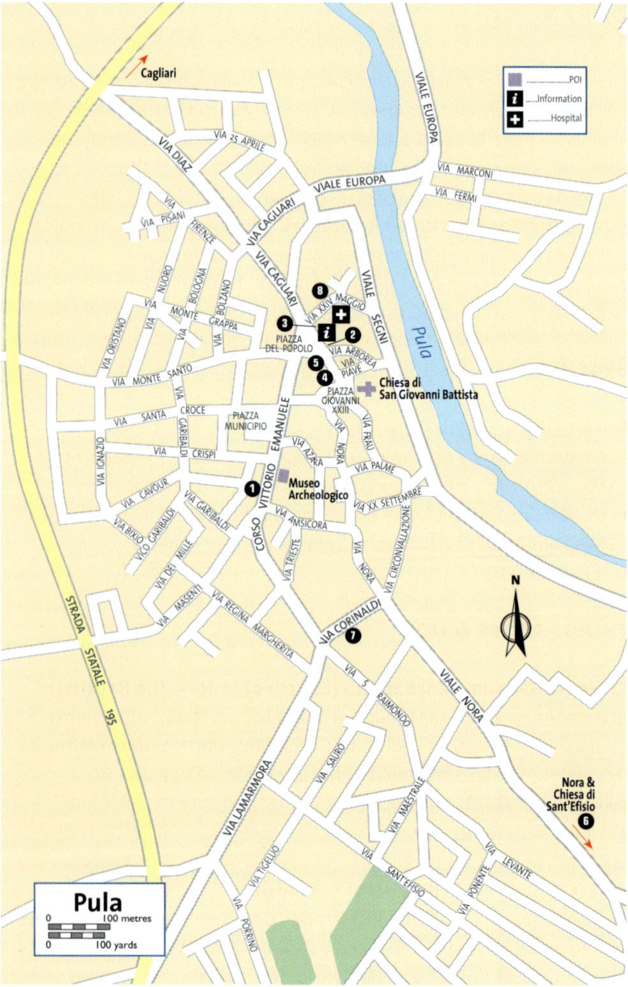
Cagliari
POI
Information
Hospital
VIALE EUROPA
VIA MARCONI
VIA FERMI
VIA 25 APRILE
VIA DIAZ
VIALE EUROPA
VIA CAGLIARI
VIA PISANI
VIA FIRENZE
VIA CAGLIARI
VIA NUORO
VIA BOLOGNA
VIA BOLZANO
VIA MONTE GRAPPA
VIA ORISTANO
VIA XXIV MAGGIO
VIALE SEGNI
Pula
PIAZZA DEL POPOLO
VIA ARBOREA
VIA PIAVE
VIA MONTE SANTO
Chiesa di San Giovanni Battista
PIAZZA GIOVANNI XXIII
VIA SANTA CROCE
PIAZZA MUNICIPIO
EMANUELE
VIA GARIBALDI
VIA CRISPI
VIA IGNAZIO
VIA AZARA
VIA NORA
VIA FRAU
VIA PALME
Museo Archeologico
VIA CAVOUR
VIA GARIBALDI
CORSO VITTORIO
VIA XX SETTEMBRE
VIA AMSICORA
VIA CIRCONVALLAZIONE
VIA BIXIO
VICO GARIBALDI
VIA DEI MILLE
VIA TRIESTE
VIA NORA
VIA MASENTI
VIA REGINA MARGHERITA
VIA CORINALDI
STRADA STATALE 195
VIA S RAIMONDO
VIALE NORA
N
VIA LAMARMORA
VIA SAURO
VIA MAESTRALE
Nora & Chiesa di Sant'Efisio
VIA LEVANTE
VIA PONENTE
VIA SANT'EFISIO
VIA TIGELLIO
VIA PORRINO
Pula
0 100 metres
0 100 yards

a procession makes the long journey from Cagliari to the church to celebrate St Ephisius, a 3rd-century Roman emissary who converted to Christianity but who was subsequently put to death as a heretic by Emperor Flavian. St Ephisius is credited with stopping a plague which hit Cagliari in the mid-16th century, since which time celebrations have been held in the capital and the procession bearing a statue of the saint has made its way to Nora.

ⓐ Nora ⓑ Open for services only

Museo Archeologico (Archaeological Museum)

Like most of Sardinia's dusty archaeological museums, this one-room collection of artefacts from Nora is not much to write home about but can put slightly more meat on the archaeological bones you have seen/will see at the site itself.

ⓐ Corso Vittorio Emanuele 67 ⓘ 070 92 09 610 ⓑ 09.00–20.00
ⓘ Admission charge; one ticket valid for museum and Nora site

Nora

The settlement of Nora, 3 km (2 miles) south of Pula, was founded around 2,800 years ago by the Phoenicians for whom it was a strategic sea port. Over time it was occupied and added to by the Carthaginians from just over the horizon in North Africa, and finally the Romans, who made it the capital of Sardinia but then abandoned the site in the 5th century due to rising sea levels. Much of the town lies submerged just off the coast, and most of what you can see on land dates from the Roman period. The small, relatively intact amphitheatre, several well-preserved Roman mosaics and a few much-photographed stone columns are the highlights of the rubble-strewn site, though with a little imagination you can also reconstruct temples, baths, warehouses and a forum in your mind's eye. Artefacts unearthed at Nora can be viewed in the archaeological museums in Pula (see above) and Cagliari (see page 18).

There are no guided tours of the ruins and visitors can explore at will (allow around 40 minutes to see everything). Atmospheric evening

RESORTS

Chiesa di Sant'Efisio is right by the beach in Nora

PULA & NORA

performances are held at the Nora amphitheatre in July and August. Ask at the tourist office for details.

❶ 070 92 09 138 ❷ 09.00–sunset ❸ Admission charge; one ticket valid for Nora site and museum in Pula

Summer concerts
From mid-June until mid-September a variety of free music performances take place almost every evening on a stage in the Piazza del Popolo. Ask at the tourist office for details.

TAKING A BREAK

Café del Corso £ ❶ This typical Italian espresso joint is conveniently situated almost opposite the museum. ⓐ Corso V Emanuele 50 ❶ 070 92 45 300 ❷ 07.00–late

L'Incontro £ ❷ The 'Encounter' is located next door to the Su Nuraghe, and advertises itself as a pizzeria and cocktail bar. Choose from a selection of over 50 reasonably priced pizzas and watch the crowds go by on Piazza del Popolo. ⓐ Piazza del Popolo ❶ 070 92 09 987 ❷ 10.00–16.00, 17.00–late

Su Nuraghe £ ❸ This large, friendly place turns into a real tourist haven when Pula is transformed into a ghost town in the heat of the afternoon. There's a self-service food bar where you can help yourself to pasta, seafood and salad which can be consumed indoors or outside on the square. Lively place for drinks in the evening. ⓐ Piazza del Popolo 57 ❶ 070 92 09 144 ❷ 05.30–late

Frederico's £–££ ❹ Informal café by day, cocktail bar by night, this relaxing place with its hefty wicker furniture and simple pasta, salad and meat menu is ideal for a light lunch or evening drinks. ⓐ Via Nora 84 ❶ 070 92 46 089 ❷ 07.00–late

RESORTS

AFTER DARK

Restaurants & bars

Mr Jingles £–££ ❺ Contemporary restaurant and cocktail bar with art nouveau flourishes and a menu of fish and steak (including horse). The two-table balcony is like the royal box for the evening concerts down on the piazza, but you'll have to book early. ⓐ Piazza del Popolo 5 ❶ 070 92 46 047 ❸ 07.00–late

Byrsa ££ ❻ Situated almost at the gates of the Nora site, this huge café, bar and restaurant is a one-stop shop for visitors to the area at any time of day. The fresh fish dishes come highly recommended, as do the sea views from the large terrace. ⓐ Località Nora ❶ 338 48 29 796 ❸ 09.00–late

Loch Ness Pub ££ ❼ Despite the name, any association with the British Isles at this brand new eatery ends at the Guinness® on tap. The menu is decidedly Sardinian with a selection of typical seafood pasta dishes and fresh fish on offer. Friendly and quite lively in the evenings.
ⓐ Via Corinaldi 23 ❶ 070 92 45 700 ❸ 10.00–16.00, 19.00–24.00

Su Furriadroxu ££ ❽ When in full swing with smoke drifting through the evening air from the open fire gently roasting a suckling pig, a band performing traditional Sardinian music and the local wine flowing unhindered, this is an unmissable place. Some English is spoken and a €15 tourist menu including drinks is available. ⓐ Via XXIV Maggio 11 ❶ 070 92 45 651 ❸ 12.30–15.00, 19.00–late

Bosa

There can be no more atmospheric or picturesque place on the island of Sardinia than the historic fishing village of Bosa. Divided between the main village 2 km (1 mile) inland and a marina where the River Temo meets the sea, this enchanting – and relatively undiscovered and isolated – place has something for everyone, sun-seekers and culture vultures alike. The village is a warren of narrow streets lined with tall tenements with washing hung between the upper floors, and lace weavers and small shops occupying ground level. The livelier marina has a wonderfully wide dark golden beach lined with bars and restaurants where the party goes on long into the night. The village also has some noteworthy historic sights such as the hilltop **Castello Malaspina (Malaspina Castle)**, a baroque cathedral and a beautiful old bridge.

THINGS TO SEE & DO

Casa Deriu (Deriu House)
Bosa's main street is a grand thoroughfare lined with mansions and small palaces. Roughly halfway along you will find the 19th-century Casa Deriu, the town's museum and an art gallery dedicated to the 20th-century Italian artist Melkiorre Melis. The museum houses a fascinating mock-up of a 19th-century interior and items relating to the tanning industry, once the mainstay of the local economy.
ⓐ Corso Vittorio Emanuele 59 ❶ 078 53 77 043 ⓛ 10.00–13.00, 16.00–18.00 Tues–Sun ❶ Admission charge

Castello Malaspina (Malaspina Castle)
Walk uphill in any direction from the old historic Sa Costa part of town and you are certain to end up at Bosa's proud hilltop castle, which has looked down on proceedings below since it was built by the Malaspina family as far back as 1112. Count on spending around an hour to explore its towers and ramparts and the small **Chiesa di Nostra Signora di**

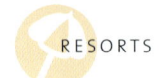

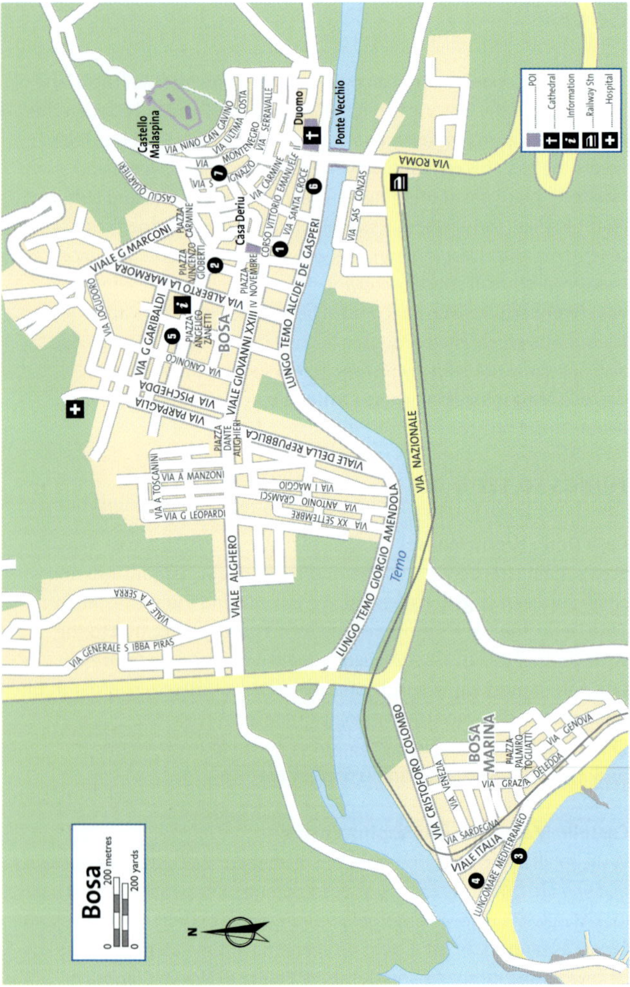
Bosa
0
200 metres
0
200 yards
N
Castello Malaspina
Duomo
Ponte Vecchio
Casa Deriu
BOSA
BOSA MARINA
Temo
VIA NINO CAN GAVINO
VIA ULTIMA COSTA
VIA MONTENEGRO
VIA SERRAVALLE
VIA S IGNAZIO
VIA CARMINE
CORSO VITTORIO EMANUELE II
VIA SANTA CROCE
VIA SAS CONZAS
VIA ROMA
CASCIU QUARTIERI
PIAZZA CARMINE
VIALE G MARCONI
PIAZZA VINCENZO GIOBERTI
PIAZZA IV NOVEMBRE
VIA ALBERTO LA MARMORA
VIA LOGUDORO
VIA G GARIBALDI
PIAZZA ANGELICO ZANETTI
VIALE GIOVANNI XXIII
LUNGO TEMO ALCIDE DE GASPERI
VIA CANONICO
VIA PISCHEDDA
VIA PARPAGLIA
PIAZZA DANTE ALIGHIERI
VIALE DELLA REPUBBLICA
VIA A TOSCANINI
VIA A MANZONI
VIA G LEOPARDI
VIA I MAGGIO
VIA ANTONIO GRAMSCI
VIA XX SETTEMBRE
VIALE ALGHERO
LUNGO TEMO GIORGIO AMENDOLA
VIA NAZIONALE
VIALE A A SERRA
VIA GENERALE S IBBA PIRAS
VIA CRISTOFORO COLOMBO
VIA VENEZIA
PIAZZA PALMIRO TOGLIATTI
VIA GENOVA
VIA GRAZIA DELEDDA
VIA SARDEGNA
VIALE ITALIA
LUNGOMARE MEDITERRANEO
POI
Cathedral
Information
Railway Stn
Hospital

> **SHOPPING**
> Walking through streets of the Sa Costa you will come across old women wedged in their doorways making lace and weaving baskets in the traditional fashion. They often have a stock of attractive items to sell to passing tourists.

Regnos Altos (Church of Our Lady of Regnos Altos), which boasts frescoes dating as far back as 1300.
Malaspina Castle @ Hilltop ⓣ 078 53 77 043 ⓒ 10.00–13.00, 15.30–18.00 Mon–Sun (Sept & Oct, Apr–June); 10.00–13.00, 16.00–19.30 Mon–Sun (July); 10.00–19.30 Mon–Sun (Aug) ⓘ Admission charge

Duomo (Cathedral)
Filling its small piazza where the Old Bridge meets Corso Vittorio Emanuele, this jumble of structures may have acquired some baroque and rococo cladding since it was built but somewhere underneath is the original 15th-century building. The interior is a riot of 18th- and 19th-century ornament.
@ Piazza Duomo

Ponte Vecchio (Old Bridge)
One of the most picturesque and photogenic sights in Bosa is the Ponte Vecchio, which even after centuries of use is still the only bridge in the main town uniting the banks of the River Temo (though there is now a new one at the marina). Cars, buses and lorries still squeeze over its narrow span. The half-derelict buildings on the other side of the river from the old town are former tanneries.

EXCURSION
Narrow-gauge railway In summer a tourist train known as *Il Trenino Verde della Sardegna* (the little green train of Sardinia) runs along a narrow-gauge railway linking Bosa Marina with Macomer, 46 km

RESORTS

⬤ *Old town, Bosa*

BOSA

(29 miles) inland. All the fun is in the scenic route and in the fact that carriages are often pulled by steam locomotives. From Macomer either return to Bosa or catch a mainline service to Cagliari or points north.
❶ Freephone 800 460 220 ❾ www.treninoverde.com

Scenic drive to Alghero

If you have your own set of wheels, the coastal drive to Alghero is one of the most spectacular on the island. The deserted 30-km (18½-mile) stretch of road ducks, dives, twists and veers its way around cliffs and promontories, and you'll certainly want to stop along the way to admire the dramatic vistas. With not one village along the route make sure you have enough petrol and take the corners carefully in wet conditions.

TAKING A BREAK

La Caffetteria £ ❶ However long you are in Bosa, you should definitely make at least one visit to this superb café housed in an 18th-century palace on the main drag. It has won awards for its coffee and is listed in the top 100 best cafés in Italy. The historic interior is spanned by a vaulted ceiling and the walls are lined with works by local artists. Live music at weekends. ⓐ Corso Vittorio Emanuele 71 ❶ 078 53 73 092 ❶ 07.00–late

Central Bar £ ❷ A simple snack bar in the modern part of Bosa serving panini, salads, ice creams, local wine and coffees which you can enjoy out on the picturesque square. ⓐ Piazza Gioberti 5 ❶ 334 35 24 09 ❶ 07.00–late

Lido Chelo £–££ ❸ Handy for a hungry beach crowd by day and frequented by all kinds of diners in the evening, the restaurant below a hotel of the same name is a modern, clean-cut affair with an international menu. ⓐ Lungomare Mediterraneo ❶ 078 53 73 804 ❶ 07.30–23.00

RESORTS

AFTER DARK

Restaurants & bars

S'hard Rock Café £ ❹ Located in a mock ship on the seafront, this fun place bedecked in American kitsch is a good place to come for a coffee or pizza during the day and a lively nightspot after dark. ⓐ Lungomare Mediterraneo ⓛ 12.30–15.00, 19.00–late

Mouse Club ££ ❺ The oddly named Mouse Club has a cosy bar area full of character and packed with pictures of yesteryear Bosa as well as a Perspex-fronted terrace on the main square in the modern part of town. Different set menu every day. ⓐ Piazza Zanetti 7 ⓛ 06.00–22.00 Mon–Fri, 06.00–01.00 Sat; closed Sun

Trattoria Sa Nassa ££ ❻ The focus is firmly on local seafood at this small, bare, stone-walled cellar eatery at the end of the Ponte Vecchio. Very popular with locals. ⓐ Via Lungo Temo 13 ⓣ 078 53 73 024 ⓛ 12.30–15.30, 17.00–22.00

Borgo Sant'Ignazio ££–£££ ❼ Sardinian seafood and pasta dishes are what you'll find on the menu at this intimate, welcoming and slightly more upmarket restaurant in the heart of the Old Town. ⓐ Via Sant'Ignazio 33 ⓣ 078 53 74 662 ⓛ 13.00–15.00, 19.30–23.00; closed Wed

Alghero

The energetic seaside town of Alghero in the northwest of the island is by far Sardinia's most engaging resort with some superb beaches, lively nightlife and tempting seafood restaurants. It comes as no surprise, therefore, that Alghero is a firm favourite among British tourists visiting the island, a situation helped along by the town's international airport, which enjoys direct budget airline connections to the UK. If it's a beach holiday with a touch of culture and great food you are seeking, look no further than Alghero, the most tourist-friendly resort in Sardinia.

The town has a decidedly Catalan flavour to it as the area was occupied by the Spanish in the 14th century. This lends it a busier, perkier, businesslike feel than can be found in other more typically Sardinian resorts. Some townspeople still speak an almost medieval version of Catalan, and most street signs bear both Catalan and Italian names. The siesta is less strictly observed here than in Cagliari or even nearby Sassari and the standard of customer service and English is far higher than in other resorts.

Away from the beaches, the main focus of tourist interest is the tightly packed old town, which juts out into the Mediterranean and is still contained on three sides by its perfectly preserved medieval town walls. The vast majority of restaurants, bars, cafés and places of interest can be found within this area.

BEACHES

Alghero's stretch of white sandy beach begins not far from the historic centre and arches northwest towards Fertilia. Occasionally, the Mediterranean currents wash ashore tonnes of seaweed (from which Alghero gets its name – *alguer* is Catalan for seaweed) which forms a slimy barrier between the sand and the turquoise waters. However, the authorities usually mobilise teams of workers very quickly to clear the offending plant mass.

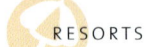

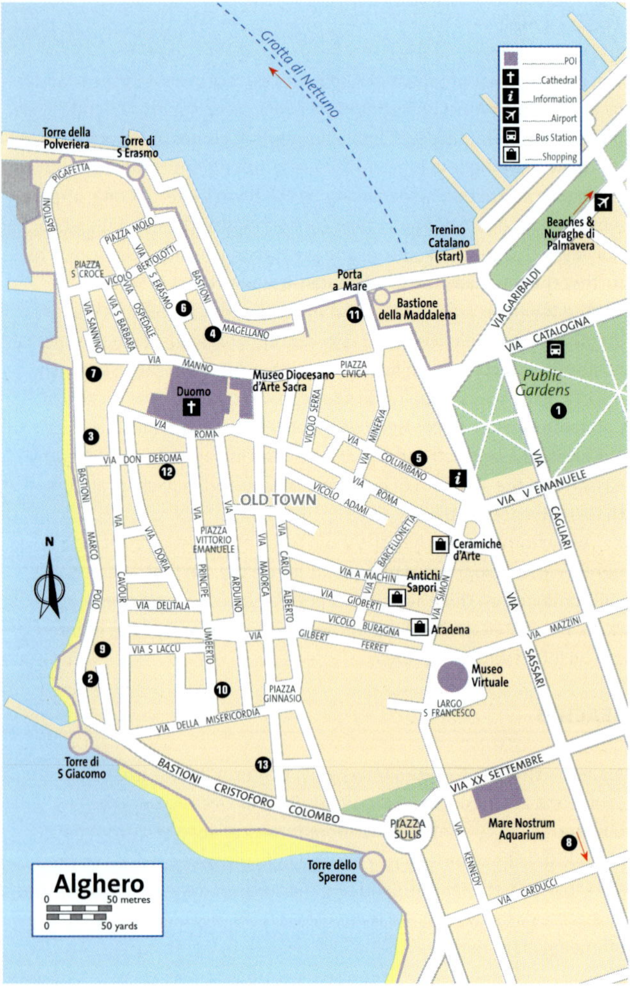
Alghero
0 50 metres
0 50 yards
POI
Cathedral
Information
Airport
Bus Station
Shopping
Grotta di Nettuno
Torre della Polveriera
Torre di S Erasmo
Trenino Catalano (start)
Beaches & Nuraghe di Palmavera
Porta a Mare
Bastione della Maddalena
Museo Diocesano d'Arte Sacra
Duomo
Public Gardens
OLD TOWN
Ceramiche d'Arte
Antichi Sapori
Aradena
Museo Virtuale
Torre di S Giacomo
Mare Nostrum Aquarium
Torre dello Sperone
PIAZZA SULIS
PIAZZA S CROCE
PIAZZA CIVICA
PIAZZA VITTORIO EMANUELE
PIAZZA GINNASIO
LARGO S FRANCESCO
PIAZZA MOLO
BASTIONI PIGAFETTA
VICOLO BERTOLOTTI
VIA S ERASMO
BASTIONI MAGELLANO
VIA SANNINO
VIA S BARBARA
VIA OSPEDALE
VIA MANNO
VIA ROMA
VICOLO SERRA
VIA MINERVA
VIA COLUMBANO
VIA DON DEROMA
VICOLO ADAMI
VIA BARCELLONETTA
VIA A MACHIN
VIA GIOBERTI
VIA SIMON
VICOLO BURAGNA
VIA GILBERT FERRET
BASTIONI MARCO POLO
VIA CAVOUR
VIA DORIA
VIA DELITALA
VIA S LACCU
VIA PRINCIPE UMBERTO
VIA ARDUINO
VIA MAJORCA
VIA CARLO ALBERTO
VIA DELLA MISERICORDIA
BASTIONI CRISTOFORO COLOMBO
VIA GARIBALDI
VIA CATALOGNA
VIA CAGLIARI
VIA V EMANUELE
VIA SASSARI
VIA MAZZINI
VIA XX SETTEMBRE
VIA KENNEDY
VIA CARDUCCI
N
1
2
3
4
5
6
7
8
9
10
11
12
13

ALGHERO

Getting around Alghero
Bus AA operates between the town centre and the airport according to the departure and arrival times of flights. A taxi costs around €20–€25.

THINGS TO SEE & DO

Duomo (Cathedral)
The cathedral bell tower dominates Alghero's skyline and the dome is a fairly impressive sight. However, the rest of the building, founded in 1510, is lost among the tightly packed tenements of the old town. Pass through the main entrance with its oversized neoclassical columns to view a mishmash of styles inside from Catalan Gothic and baroque to Moorish and neoclassical.
- Piazza Duomo Bell tower guided tours: 19.00–21.30 Tues, Thur, Sat (July & Aug); 17.00–20.00 Tues, Thur, Sat (Sept)

Mare Nostrum Aquarium (Aquarium)
The 45 tanks at Sardinia's only aquarium hold an interesting selection of predominantly Mediterranean fish, invertebrates and turtles, including seahorses, piranhas and a few sharks.
- Via XX Settembre 1 079 97 83 33 www.aquariumalghero.it
- 10.00–13.00, 15.00–20.00 (Apr & May); 10.00–13.00, 16.00–21.00 (June & Oct); 10.00–13.00, 17.00–23.00 (July & Sep); 10.00–13.30, 17.00–00.30 (Aug); 15.00–20.00 Sat, 10.00–13.00, 15.00–20.00 Sun (Nov–Mar)
- Admission charge

Museo Diocesano d'Arte Sacra (Diocese Museum of Sacred Art)
A few steps across the cobbled square stands this museum packed with precious religious treasures from the cathedral next door to it.
- La Chiesa del Rosario, Piazza Duomo 079 97 33 041
- 10.00–12.30, 18.00–21.00; closed Jan–Mar
- Admission charge

RESORTS

Museo Virtuale (Virtual Museum)
Housed in the Torre San Giovanni, once part of the inland stretch of the town walls, this interactive museum tells the story of Alghero's history in an engaging fashion.

ⓐ Torre San Giovanni, Largo San Francesco ⓣ 079 97 34 045
ⓛ 11.00–13.00, 18.00–21.00 (June & Sept); 11.00–13.00, 19.00–22.00 (July & Aug); 10.00–13.00, 17.00–19.00 (Oct–Mar) ⓘ Admission charge

● *The cathedral's bell tower dominates Alghero's old town*

Nuraghe di Palmavera
This Nuraghic site is worth a half an hour's exploration if you happen to be passing by on the road out to Neptune's Grotto. The prehistoric settlement has a relatively well-preserved central limestone tower with the remains of numerous circular dwellings spreading out from it in all directions.
ⓐ Fertilia ⓛ 09.00–19.00 Apr–Oct; 10.00–14.00 Nov–Mar
ⓘ Admission charge

Town walls
Though the land-facing defensive walls were demolished in the 19th century, the ring of stone facing the sea was spared. Interspersed with seven beefy *torre* (towers), the ramparts are pleasant places to stroll and relax with various eateries often spreading their tables along the top of the walls. The views out to sea, especially at sunset, can be exquisite.

Trenino Catalano (Little Catalan Train)
In the summer heat or during a bout of intense laziness, why not take Alghero's Dotto Train (or Little Catalan Train as it is known here), which traces a route around most of the city's major sights. An entertaining way of showing the children a little history.

> **SHOPPING**
> **Aradena** Genuine Sardinian arts and crafts direct from rural producers. If you are after top-quality rugs, knives, jewellery, glassware, etc., this is the place to come. ⓐ Via Gioberti 24/28 ⓣ 079 97 35 058 ⓛ 10.00–13.00, 16.00–late
> **Antichi Sapori** A one-stop shop for Sardinian wines, spirits, honey, cheese, bread and much more. ⓐ Via Simon 2 ⓣ 079 97 58 14 ⓛ 09.30–21.30
> **Ceramiche d'Arte** The place to purchase traditional pottery in all shapes, colours and sizes. ⓐ Via Simon 32 ⓣ 079 97 33 025 ⓛ 10.00–13.00, 16.00–late

RESORTS

○ *Houses at the edge of Alghero's fortified port*

ALGHERO

🌐 www.miras.it 🕐 Departs every 30 minutes from the harbour between 10.00–13.00, 15.30–21.00 (Apr, June & Sept); 10.00–13.00, 16.30–23.00 (July & Aug)

EXCURSIONS
Grotta di Nettuno (Neptune's Grotto)
The most popular excursion from Alghero is to Neptune's Grotto located on Capo Caccia 15 km (9¼ miles) west across the bay as the crow flies. If you don't have a hire car, the easiest way (and outside the tourist season the only way) to reach this amazing cave complex with its forest of stalagmites and stalactites and subterranean lake is to take a boat trip from Alghero harbour. Some of the curious formations illuminated with electric lighting are simply breathtaking, and a visit is for many the highlight of their trip to Sardinia. Guided tours leave every hour and take around 45 minutes.

📍 Capo Caccia ☎ 079 94 65 40 🕐 09.00–19.00 (Apr–Sept); 10.00–17.00 (Oct); 09.00–14.00 (Nov–Mar) ❶ Admission charge

TAKING A BREAK

Giardini Pubblici (Public Gardens) £ ❶ Alghero boasts many a picnic spot along the sea-facing city walls but shade can be difficult to come by. The trees of the Giardini Pubblici near the tourist information centre provide respite from the blazing sun. They also host a children's playground and a couple of good cafés. 📍 Via Cagliari

Gelateria I Bastioni £ ❷ Choose from 40 different flavours at this conveniently located ice cream parlour. 📍 Bastioni Marco Polo 5

Angedras ££ ❸ This sea-view restaurant (its name spells 'Sardegna' backwards) offers a daily menu of traditional Sardinian seafood dishes which can be enjoyed atop the town walls or in the contemporary interior. Attentive service. 📍 Bastioni Marco Polo 41 ☎ 079 97 35 078 🌐 www.angedrasrestaurant.it 🕐 12.30–14.00, 19.30–23.00

RESORTS

Caffè Latino ££ ❹ Located on a wide section of the ramparts, this popular hangout with its cosy, exposed-stone and candle-lit interior, white linen and wicker seating outside, plus its menu of drinks and snacks, is good for a relaxing refuel any time of day. ⓐ Bastioni Magellano 10 ⓣ 079 97 65 41 ⓛ 09.00–02.00

El Pultal ££ ❺ With its tightly packed benches, convivial atmosphere, huge meat, fish and pizza menu and kitschy décor, this magical backstreet eatery could be nowhere else but Italy. ⓐ Via Columbano 40 ⓣ 079 97 47 20 ⓛ 12.30–15.00, 19.30–24.00

Il Viceré ££–£££ ❻ Almost filling a tiny square a few steps from the town walls, this recommended eatery enjoys a great location and serves up a limited menu of seafood dishes. The Catalan lobster here costs a whopping €170 per kg! ⓐ Via S. Erasmo 14 ⓣ 079 59 00 786 ⓛ 12.00–15.00, 19.30–24.00

AFTER DARK

Restaurants & bars
Miques de Mirall ❼ See and be seen at this chilled-out cocktail bar and disco with its snakeskin stools, flamingo-orange walls and well-stocked bar. ⓐ Piazza Manno 14 ⓣ 3475 844 475 ⓛ 18.00–02.00 Mon–Sat

Siesta ❽ One of the best nightspots in town with an outdoor covered dance floor occupied by a throng of Alghero's young, rich and beautiful out to have a good time. ⓐ Loc. Scala Piccida ⓣ 347 39 06 965 ⓦ www.lasiestadisco.net

King's Pub £ ❾ The Brit pub knick-knackery is kept to a minimum at this simple watering hole where you can tuck into some munchies-relieving panini at 01.00 or watch a bit of satellite TV over a local Ichnusa lager. ⓐ Via Cavour 123 ⓣ 079 97 96 50 ⓛ 09.30–02.00

ALGHERO

Casablanca £–££ ⓘ This establishment is what every holidaymaker wants from an Italian restaurant – four intimate dining rooms where you rub shoulders with fellow diners, a wide range of traditional Sardinian and Italian dishes at reasonable prices and a convivial atmosphere.
ⓐ Via Principe Umberto 76 ⓣ 079 98 33 53 ⓒ 12.30–14.30, 19.30–22.30

Nettuno ££ ⓘ Apart from the excellent seafood and reasonably priced pizzas, the real highlight of the Nettuno is the terrace affording unparalleled views out to sea. ⓐ Via Maddalenetta 4 ⓣ 079 97 97 74
ⓒ 12.00–15.00, 19.00–24.00

Al Vecchio Mulino ££ ⓘ Hungry sightseers can do a lot worse than fill empty bellies with the reasonably priced pizzas and Sardinian pasta dishes here, served up under the arched vaulting of a typical Alghero town house. ⓐ Via Don Deroma 3 ⓣ 079 97 72 54
ⓦ www.alvecchiomulinoalghero.com ⓒ 12.30–15.00, 19.00–late

Al Tuguri £££ ⓘ Possibly the most authentic eatery in town occupies three floors of a 15th-century townhouse and is run by one of the island's favourite restaurateurs, Benito Carbonella. Revived seafood recipes of yesteryear and catch of the day populate the reassuringly short menu. Despite the name, which translates as 'the hovels', this has become quite a celebrity haunt, and even Madonna has eaten here. ⓐ Via Maiorca 113
ⓣ 079 97 67 72 ⓦ www.altuguri.it ⓒ 12.30–15.00, 19.00–22.30 Mon–Sat
ⓘ Reservations recommended

RESORTS

▲ *View of Torre Falcone from La Pelosa beach*

Stintino

The village of Stintino, occupying a slice of land between two small harbours, looks east across the Golfo dell'Asinara. It is inhabited by the descendants of those forced off Asinara Island to the north in the 19th century when it became a prison.

Stintino is a quiet affair at the best of times, and most of the tanning and tourist action take place 3 km (2 miles) further up the road at La Pelosa beach, one of Sardinia's best, where most of the large hotel complexes and villas congregate. However, the village is the best place to eat or join a boat tour to Asinara (no longer a penal colony), and the local **Museo della Tonnara (Tuna Museum)** constitutes a minor diversion, if only a fleeting one.

BEACHES

The beach at **La Pelosa** is one of Sardinia's most stunning. Set against the backdrop of the Spanish-era **Torre Falcone (Falcon Tower)** on tiny Piana Island just offshore, its shimmering white sand and shallow waters of indescribable shades of emerald and turquoise are jaw-droppingly beautiful.

❶ A minibus links Stintino with La Pelosa every hour in summer

THINGS TO SEE & DO

Diving
The clear waters around La Pelosa and Asinara Island provide excellent conditions for diving. The best place to contact about equipment rental is the Roccaruja Diving Centre based in a timber shack on La Pelosa beach. The centre runs PADI courses as well as windsurfing and sailing instruction.

ⓐ La Pelosa ❶ 079 52 70 06 Ⓦ www.windsurfingcenter.it

RESORTS

Museo della Tonnara (Tuna Museum)
Stintino's only tourist sight as such is the modest Museo della Tonnara housed in a pink Portakabin on the harbourside of the Porto Mannu. The six rooms trace the life of the tuna until its final bloody demise at the hands of the local fishermen.
ⓐ Porto Mannu ⓑ 18.00–24.00 Tues–Sun (summer)
❶ Admission charge

EXCURSIONS
Boat trips to Asinara Island
Asinara Island has been a national park since 1997 and is rated as one of the most unspoilt environments in the Mediterranean. After housing a prison camp during World War I, it then served as a prison for the most dangerous of criminals until 1997, and hence was out of bounds for tourists. The absence of humans meant that the island's natural flora and fauna flourished. This precious environment has now been recognised and put under official state protection. Visitors are only permitted to visit certain parts of the 16-km (10-mile) long island, and while you are not likely to see many of the wild boar, turtles, albino donkeys and wild goats that roam Asinara, the scenery and secluded beaches are worth the ride.

Asinara Charter Services Daily departures aboard a wonderful little boat called the *Cassiopea*.
ⓐ Portu Minori ❶ 079 50 80 42 ⓦ www.asinaracharterservice.com

Linea del Parco Full day Jeep tours of the island.
ⓐ Kiosk at Portu Mannu (next to Tuna Museum) ❶ 079 52 31 18

La Nassa Trips to Asinara as well as many other services for tourists including bookings, car and cycle hire and fax/internet at their handy office.
ⓐ Via Tonnara 35 ❶ 079 52 00 60 ⓦ www.stintinoincoming.com & www.escursioniasinara.it

TAKING A BREAK

Gabbiano £ Another relatively cheap and cheerful option with a large outdoor covered dining area, an ample choice of fish, meat and pasta plus 30 types of pizza. ⓐ Loc. Capo Falcone, La Pelosa ⓣ 079 52 70 89 ⓛ 12.30–15.00, 19.30–23.00

Ginepri £ Hungry beachcombers can head for this convenient forest of red and yellow plastic garden furniture just back from the beach to enjoy simple panini, meat dishes and salads. ⓐ La Pelosa ⓣ 079 52 72 46 ⓛ 08.00–20.00

Lu Fanali £–££ Munch on seafood and pizzas or just sip an espresso at this contemporary restaurant and adjoining snack bar with pretty harbour views. ⓐ Lungomare Colombo 89 ⓣ 079 52 30 54 ⓛ 07.30–24.00

AFTER DARK

Restaurants
Pininoteca Skipper £ This rarest of finds, an Italian fast food joint open 24/7, is a welcome cheap eat retreat when most restaurateurs are taking their afternoon snooze. Panini, pizzas, burgers and an €11 tourist menu as well as dazzling sea views. ⓐ Lungomare Colombo 57 ⓛ Non-stop

Da Antonio £–££ Fill up on meat, fish and pasta at this cosy eatery with tightly packed tables and reasonable prices. ⓐ Via Marco Polo 14 ⓣ 079 52 30 77 ⓛ 12.00–15.00, 19.00–23.00

La Pelosetta ££ This huge pizzeria belongs to a hotel of the same name. In addition to around 30 types of pizza they also serve a limited number of fish and meat dishes and a wide selection of quality wines. ⓐ La Pelosa ⓣ 079 527140 ⓛ 12.00–15.30, 19.00–late

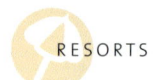

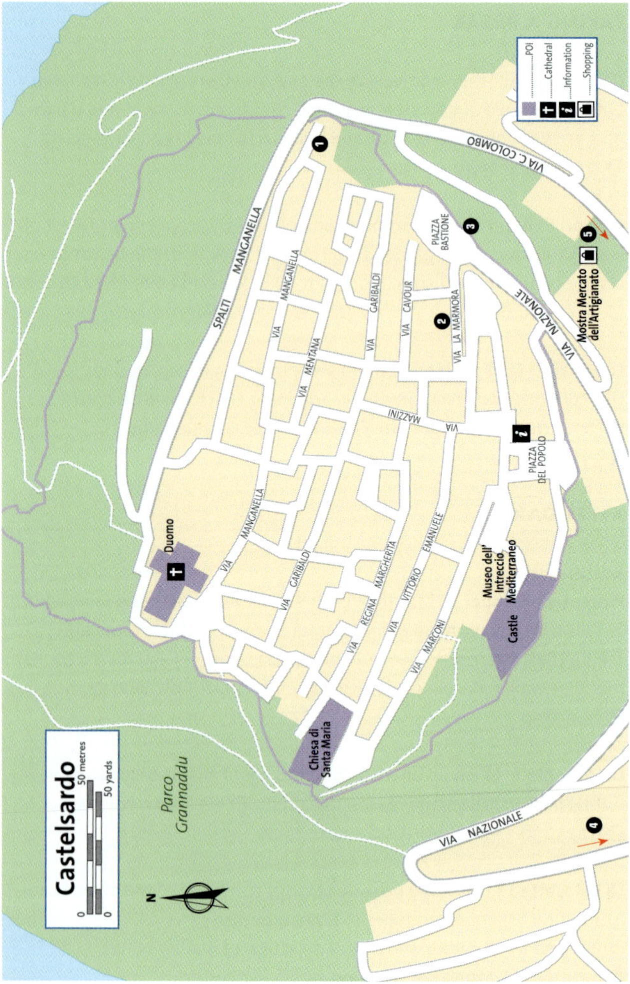
Castelsardo
0
50 metres
0
50 yards
N
Parco Grannaddu
Duomo
Chiesa di Santa Maria
Castle
Museo dell' Intreccio Mediterraneo
PIAZZA DEL POPOLO
PIAZZA BASTIONE
SPALTI MANGANELLA
VIA MANGANELLA
VIA GARIBALDI
VIA CAVOUR
VIA LA MARMORA
VIA MENTANA
VIA MAZZINI
VIA REGINA MARGHERITA
VIA VITTORIO EMANUELE
VIA MARCONI
VIA NAZIONALE
VIA C. COLOMBO
Mostra Mercato dell'Artigianato
1
2
3
4
5
POI
Cathedral
Information
Shopping

Castelsardo

Few places in Sardinia are more picturesque than the town of Castelsardo on the island's north coast. Occupying a cone of rock jutting out into the sea, the tight medieval maze of streets lined with pastel town houses are crowned by a proud castle and form one of Sardinia's most recognisable vistas when viewed from the coast.

The town has a couple of interesting historic sights but the best fun is to be had wandering the old town's warren of cobbled lanes, flights of steps, tiny squares and courtyards where the midday air is fragrant with garlic and basil. Basket weaving is the town's traditional craft and colourful items with distinctive designs can be found on sale in doorways in almost every street. The nearby beach at Lu Bagnu and Castelsardo's many authentic dining options make the town an engaging little holiday resort and day-trip destination.

BEACHES

Lu Bagnu, 5 km (3 miles) west of Castelsardo, is the nearest beach of any size. Regular buses make the run. Apart from the sandy strand there's not a lot else to this modern mini-resort.

THINGS TO SEE & DO

Chiesa di Santa Maria (Church of St Mary)

Tucked away in a far corner of the old town, this is a simple Gothic structure, little changed since Catalan times. The baroque altars inside liven things up slightly and the cool interior is a tranquil place to escape the sun and crowds. The church's pride and joy is a precious black crucifix called the Black Christ dating from the 14th century.

ⓐ Via Vittorio Emanuele 🕒 09.00–19.30

RESORTS

Duomo (Cathedral)
Dominated by an octagonal campanile with its colourful tiled roof, Castelsardo's main place of worship has stood on this site since Gothic times, though it was rebuilt in the 16th century and some baroque baubles were added two centuries later. Many come here to see the Madonna with Angels, a 15th-century work by the so-called Maestro di Castelsardo. Visitors can also descend into the crypt containing an exhibition of religious art.

ⓐ Via Manganella ⓣ 079 47 11 42 ⓛ 08.30–19.30

Mostra Mercato dell'Artigianato (Handicrafts Supermarket)
Worth a mention for its sheer size – the biggest souvenir emporium you'll ever see, occupying 2,000 sq m (about 21,500 sq ft)! Cork, ceramics, tapestries, basketwork, coral and a whole host of other knick-knacks.

ⓐ Via Roma 15/17 ⓣ 079 47 10 61 ⓛ 09.00–22.00

Museo dell'Intreccio Mediterraneo (Mediterranean Basket Weaving Museum)
The castle which gave Castelsardo its name has sat high above the town since 1102 when it was built by the powerful Doria family. It now houses a basketwork and weaving museum containing fine examples of dishes, bowls and even a boat woven by local craftsmen from dwarf palm leaves.

ⓐ Castello del Doria, Via Marconi ⓣ 079 47 13 80 ⓛ 09.00–13.00, 15.00–21.00 (June & Sept); 09.00–13.00, 15.00–24.00 (July & Aug); 09.30–13.00, 15.00–17.00 (Oct–May) ⓘ Admission charge

> **SHOPPING**
>
> Every second or third shop in Castelsardo is a souvenir outlet selling everything from made-in-China plastic key rings to authentic Castelsardo basketwork. As mentioned on page 51, locally woven items are on sale direct from the producers all around town.

CASTELSARDO

▲ *The picturesque town of Castelsardo is crowned by its castle*

RESORTS

TAKING A BREAK

Aragona £ ❶ If all you need is a relaxing place to sit, admire the view and take a little light lunch of honestly prepared, simple Italian pastas, panini and meat dishes, go no further than this friendly little place in the northeast corner of the old part of town. ⓐ Via Manganella 1 ⓣ 079 47 00 81 ⓛ 12.00–15.00, 19.00–late

Bounty ££ ❷ One of the best restaurants in the old part of town specialising in traditional pasta and seafood dishes. They also stock a huge selection of exclusively Sardinian wines. ⓐ Via La Marmora 12 ⓣ 079 47 90 43 ⓛ 12.00–15.00, 19.00–24.00

AFTER DARK

La Guardiola ££ ❸ The stupendous views from the alfresco dining area, an extensive menu, the location just below the castle and English-speaking waiters make this one of the best places to eat in town. ⓐ Piazza Bastione 4 ⓣ 079 47 04 28 ⓛ 12.00–15.00, 19.00–24.00

Hotel Nadir ££ ❹ The dining room on the fifth floor of the Hotel Nadir on the Lu Bagnu road has some of the best views in town. Enjoy the fixed menu for €29 while admiring the sea and Castelsardo's hilltop location framed in the large windows. Pity it doesn't open more often! ⓐ Via Lungomare Anglona ⓣ 079 47 02 97 ⓛ 20.00–24.00 Wed–Sun and lunchtime July & Aug

Il Cormorano £££ ❺ This is one of Castelsardo's more upmarket affairs with an interior decorated in traditional tapestries and tiles, neatly laid tables, a shady terrace and a menu dominated by local fish and lobster. ⓐ Via C. Colombo 5 ⓣ 079 47 06 28 ⓛ 13.00–15.00, 20.00–late

Porto Cervo

The Costa Smeralda (Emerald Coast) is a name used to describe 10 km (6 miles) of coves, bays and beaches dotted with a series of very exclusive resorts in the northeast of the island. Now the haunt of the rich and famous yacht-owning set, this once wild and virtually uninhabited stretch of coastline was 'discovered' by the Aga Khan in 1958 while on a yachting trip. With a posse of investors and developers behind him, he set about buying up the land and creating resorts such as Porto Cervo, a playground for the super-rich glitterati.

The villas of Porto Cervo are set in grand and impeccably maintained surroundings. The town consists of an elite shopping centre with a wide variety of designer names on show, moorings for super-size yachts and a couple of pricey eateries. Porto Cervo is therefore not ideal for people on any kind of budget.

Unless you're a member of the paparazzi there's little to point a camera at in Porto Cervo, though some of the pastel-coloured pseudo-Moorish architecture and the **Chiesa di Stella Maris (Church of Stella Maris)** are something a bit different. In summer there is a bustling atmosphere around the marina, though the town is quiet out of season. The understated ambience and crime- and litter-free streets are attractive features of this upmarket resort.

BEACHES

There are no beaches in Porto Cervo itself. For some bucket-and-spade fun head south to Cala di Volpe or north to Baia Sardinia.

SHOPPING

ISOLA A branch of ISOLA selling Sardinian handicrafts can be found in the Sottopiazza. ⓐ Sottopiazza ⓣ 0789 944 28 ⓛ 09.00–13.00, 15.00–19.00 Mon–Fri, 09.00–13.00 Sat

RESORTS

THINGS TO SEE & DO

Chiesa di Stella Maris (Church of Stella Maris)
The almost surreal whitewashed architecture of this church dominating the hillside opposite the marina is modern architecture at its best. It was built in 1968 according to a design by the same architect responsible for the town's shopping complex. There's hardly a straight line in the building with the wavy façade hanging onto a bell tower, which looks like the plasticine handiwork of a child. The roof of the porch, which extends along the entire front of the building, is supported by huge chunks of oddly worn rock, the form and texture of which are a common phenomenon in this part of Sardinia. The interior is a pleasingly simple affair, the air scented by the local juniper wood used for the furniture. A painting by El Greco called the *Mater Dolorosa* donated by a Dutch nobleman hangs in the church.
ⓐ Via Stella Maris

Piazzetta & Sottopiazza
The Piazzetta is a tiny, purpose-built square lined with exclusive boutiques and a couple of cafés where you can easily drink away your holiday euros in one evening. Down a couple of flights of steps you enter the Sottopiazza, an irregular warren of exclusive shopping experiences with some high-flying outlets displaying sky-high prices.

TAKING A BREAK

La Virgola £–££ A modern friendly place in the Sottopiazza selling coffees, snacks and homemade ice cream for just over the normal prices you'd pay elsewhere in Sardinia. ⓐ Portici Sottopiazza ⓣ 0789 920 98 ⓛ 08.30–24.00 (Easter–Oct)

Café du Port ££ This superb restaurant is one of the best places to eat fresh pasta, sip a cocktail, rub shoulders with celebrities and watch the sun set over the yachts in the old harbour. ⓐ Vecchio Molo ⓣ 0789 923 84 ⓛ 07.00–late (Apr–Nov)

Glamour Café £££ Possibly the priciest café on the island with central London prices but without the service to match. 'Enjoy' wildly overpriced cocktails and coffee in the outdoor seating area, which almost fills the tiny Piazzetta. ⓐ Piazzetta degli Archi ⓣ 0789 909 009 ⓛ 07.30–22.00

AFTER DARK

Restaurants

Il Pepperone ££ At this al fresco restaurant on the main road behind the Piazzatta, pizzas cost twice as much as in Cagliari and, somewhat surprisingly in this the haunt of the international jet set, the waiters speak *solo Italiano*. ⓐ Via della Cerbiatta ⓣ 0789 907 049 ⓦ www.ilpeperone.com ⓛ 12.30–late

La Petronilla ££–£££ Treat your taste buds to some traditional fare in the small dining room of this little piece of Sardinia in Porto Cervo. ⓐ Località Sa ConCa 42 ⓣ 0789 921 37 ⓦ www.lapetronilla.com ⓛ Evenings ⓘ Reservations are advised

● *Chiesa di Stella Maris*

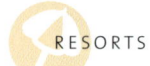

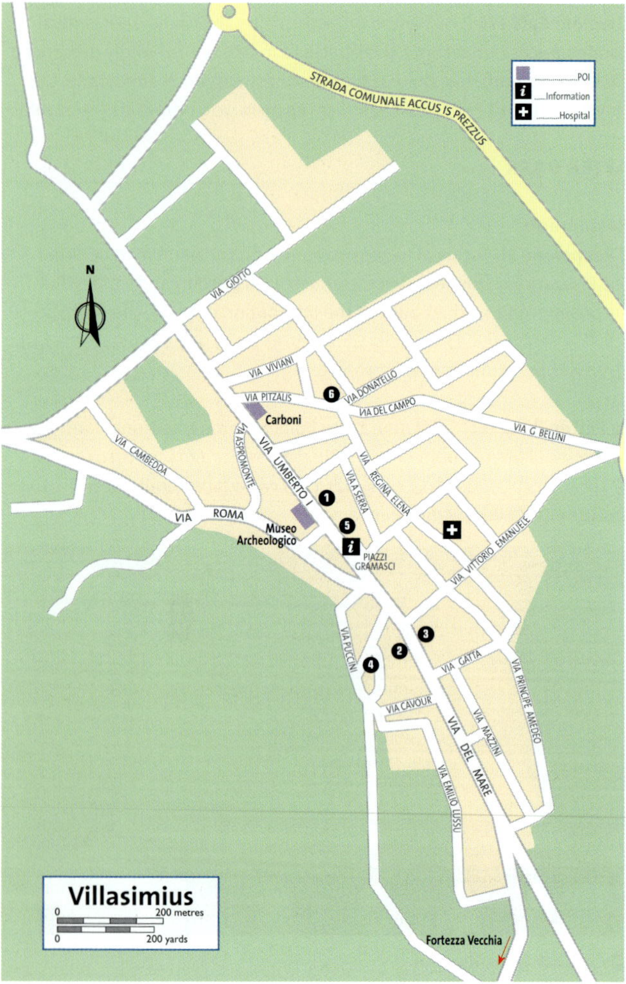
Villasimius
0
200 metres
0
200 yards
N
POI
Information
Hospital
STRADA COMUNALE ACCUS IS PREZZUS
VIA GIOTTO
VIA VIVIANI
VIA PITZALIS
VIA DONATELLO
VIA DEL CAMPO
VIA G BELLINI
Carboni
VIA CAMBEDDA
VIA ASPROMONTE
VIA UMBERTO I
VIA A SERRA
VIA REGINA ELENA
VIA ROMA
Museo
Archeologico
PIAZZI
GRAMASCI
VIA VITTORIO EMANUELE
VIA PUCCINI
VIA GATTA
VIA CAVOUR
VIA DEL MARE
VIA MAZZINI
VIA PRINCIPE AMEDEO
VIA EMILIO LUSSU
Fortezza Vecchia
1
2
3
4
5
6

Villasimius

This busy resort about 35 km (22 miles) east of Cagliari on the southeastern tip of Sardinia thrives on tourism in the summer season. It is the ideal retreat for those looking for superb beaches, fine seafood restaurants, and light hiking and cycling possibilities. The town is situated around 3 km (2 miles) from the Med at the land end of the Capo Carbonara with its old fortress, marina, sheltered sandy bays and wetlands inhabited by flamingos in the winter months.

BEACHES

The secluded rocky coves and shimmering strands of the Capo Carbonara are the real reason sun-seekers travel to Sardinia's sizzling southeast. The nearest stretch of sand to the town lies around 2 km (1 mile) to the south at Simius, while the popular Spiaggia del Riso can be found around 3 km (2 miles) to the southwest. With a car you can reach the Costa Rei to the north with its kilometres of deserted sand-fringed shoreline.

THINGS TO SEE & DO

Fortezza Vecchia (Old Fortress)
The square block of the Fortezza Vecchia dates from the 17th century and was built to protect Villasimius from pirate raids. Nowadays it is put to good use as an art exhibition venue. Ask at the tourist office or call ahead to find out what's on.
ⓐ Capo Carbonara ⓣ 070 79 30 232 ⓞ 10.00–13.00, 18.00–21.00 Fri–Wed (June–Sept); 10.00–13.00, 15.00–17.00 Fri–Sun (Oct–May)
❶ Admission charge

Museo Archeologico (Archaeological Museum)
Villasimius's dusty collection of artefacts unearthed during digs in the surrounding area is only of interest to those with a dedicated passion for the island's ancient history.

RESORTS

(a) Via Frau 5 (t) 070 793 02 90 (L) 10.00–13.00 Tues–Thur, 10.00–13.00, 17.00–19.00 Fri–Sun (mid-Sept–mid-June); 10.00–13.00, 21.00–midnight Tues–Sun (mid-June–mid-Sept) (!) Admission charge

EXCURSION

The Carboni travel agency is a one-stop shop for trips, car and motorbike hire, tourist information, and all other bookings and information in the area. They can arrange sightseeing flights, quad-bike excursions, *trenino verde* (little green train) rides, boat trips, guided tours of Villasimius and even day trips to Cagliari. **Carboni** (a) Via Umberto I 122 (t) 070 79 10 09 (w) www.laviadelmare.com (L) 09.00–13.00, 16.30–20.00

TAKING A BREAK

La Gelateria di Sartori £ ❶ A traditional gelato joint selling myriad flavours in all the colours of the rainbow. (a) Via Umberto I 60 (t) 070 79 03 41 (L) 10.00–23.00 (until last customer leaves in summer)

La Galleria ££ ❷ This enormous place just off the main square houses a café, a pizzeria, a restaurant and a rooftop terrace with views of the surrounding craggy hinterland, all spread out over four floors. It is good for a quick espresso, a romantic dinner or a pasta and pizza blow-out. There's live music every Saturday night and the siesta here is a thing of the past. (a) Via Umberto I (t) 070 79 20 68 (L) 11.00–03.00

AFTER DARK

Restaurants & bars
Plaza Café ❸ This nautical-theme bar is by far the best place in town to sip a cocktail or beer, people-watch and enjoy the balmy summer evening air. (a) Piazza Incani 1 (t) 070 79 28 019 (L) 19.00–late

Al Vecchio Faro £–££ ❹ Ravioli with potato and mint, *malloreddus*, soft cheese and honey dessert and local wines are just some of the delights

◐ *Colourful beach scene at Villasimius*

of this friendly and down-to-earth restaurant where the focus is very much on local food of the highest quality. There are also more than 20 different types of pizza to choose from. ⓐ Via Puccini 6 ⓣ 070 79 13 68 ⓛ 12.30–15.00, 18.30–late

Carbonara ££ ❺ Villasimius's finest seafood restaurant boasts a marine theme throughout, a mixed Italian and traditional Sardinian menu and an aquarium from which you can select an unsuspecting sea creature as your main course. ⓐ Via Umberto I 54 ⓛ 12.30–14.45, 20.00–22.00

Il Giardino ££ ❻ The airy contemporary interior here sits in contrast with the traditional Sardinian menu. There is a pleasant terrace and the staff speak some English. A bit of a hike from the immediate town centre but worth it. ⓐ Via Brunelleschi 4 ⓣ 070 79 14 41 ⓛ 12.00–15.00, 18.30–24.00

◐ *Sassari is Sardinia's second-largest city*

EXCURSIONS
Out & about

EXCURSIONS

Sassari

Proud Sassari is Sardinia's second city and the capital of the northwest Sassari Province. If you've had your fill of lounging around by the sea in Alghero or Stintino, the city makes for a straightforward day trip, providing a taste of inland Sardinia and something a little different. Many may find themselves here between bus and train connections when travelling around the island, as Sassari is a major transport hub for the north.

A section of the city centre is a medieval maze of narrow lanes and squares dotted with churches and Renaissance architecture. The baroque **Duomo di San Nicola (Cathedral of St Nicholas)** and the **Chiesa di Santa Maria di Betlem (Church of St Mary of Bethlehem)**, the **Museo Nazionale Archeologico ed Etnografico 'G.A. Sanna' (National Archaeological and Ethnographic Museum)** and grand **Piazza Italia** are the main places of interest. What's more, there are plenty of restaurants. Some of these serve up some interesting cuts of meat (horse and donkey), the food of the interior and a far cry from the pizza-pasta onslaught of the coastal resorts.

THINGS TO SEE & DO

Chiesa di Santa Maria di Betlem (Church of St Mary of Bethlehem)
This church is located next to the bus station on Piazza Santa Maria. The Romanesque façade conceals a baroque interior lined with chapels dedicated to various trades (tailors, carpenters, etc.). The huge wooden candle-like objects stored in the church are the stars of the show at the city's **I Candelieri** festival (see page 102) held annually in mid-August.
ⓐ Piazza Santa Maria

Duomo di San Nicola (Cathedral of St Nicholas)
One of the highlights of a tour of Sassari must be the intricately carved stonework of the Duomo's façade whose grandeur stands in stark

SASSARI

○ *Chiesa di Santa Maria di Betlem*

EXCURSIONS

> **GETTING THERE**
> Sassari has a large railway station where trains from all over the island call. There are direct mainline connections to Olbia, Oristano, Cagliari and Porto Torres. A quaint narrow-gauge railway, the only one to operate as a normal service year round, winds its way to Alghero with the miniature trains making the trip both ways around 11 times a day. Sassari also has coach connections to most towns in the north of the island.

contrast to the decaying streets radiating from the square it dominates. It's the finest piece of baroque cladding on the island, but is only skin-deep as the interior is a plain Gothic affair.
ⓐ Piazza Duomo 🕒 09.00–12.00, 16.00–19.00

Fontana del Rosello (Rosello Fountain)
This easily overlooked Renaissance fountain is tucked away behind the **Chiesa della Trinità (Church of the Trinity)** in Corso Trinità down a flight of overgrown cobbled steps. The wonderfully carved square monument dates from 1606 and is supplied by a spring, which was once the city's sole water supply.
ⓐ Corso Trinità

Museo Nazionale Archeologico ed Etnografico 'G.A. Sanna' (National Archaeological and Ethnographic Museum)
This large museum and Sassari's principal tourist attraction is the best museum outside of Cagliari and will even hold the attention of those with little interest in Sardinia's history. The collections contain artefacts from all periods of human activity on the island including prehistoric tools and weapons, Carthaginian jewellery and vases, Roman mosaics, pottery and numerous finds from Sardinia's unique Nuraghic sites (see page 77). There's also a small section on medieval Sassari featuring a scale model of the town when it was still encircled by hefty defensive

walls. On the ground floor there is a small gallery exhibiting art by local painters dating from the 14th to the 20th centuries.
ⓐ Via Roma 64 ⓣ 079 27 22 03 ⓦ www.museosannasassari.it
ⓞ 09.00–20.00 Tues–Sun ⓘ Admission charge

Piazza Italia
Sassari's finest square to the east of the historic core is where you'll find two of the city's most impressive buildings. The entire northeastern flank is dominated by the perfectly symmetrical late 19th-century **Palazzo della Provincia**, seat of the provincial authorities. Facing it across the cobbles is the impressive neo-Gothic **Palazzo Giordano** and between the two stands the statue of a grumpy-looking King Vittorio Emanuele II flanked by an ensemble of palm trees. The whole square was recently renovated and restored to its former glory.

TAKING A BREAK

Giardini Pubblici (Public Gardens) Sassari, to its credit, has a fine set of well-pruned public gardens where you can picnic on iron benches in the shade. A fountain plays in one half, children in the other on a collection of slides and swings. ⓐ Margherita di Savoia (opposite the university)

SHOPPING
Corso Vittorio Emanuele II Long and cobbled, this shopping thoroughfare climbs from just north of the railway station to Piazza Italia. It is lined with small boutiques and shops selling everything from Gucci to gas cylinders.
ISOLA A large ISOLA outlet occupies one corner of the Giardini Pubblici (Public Gardens) and sells a wide selection of traditional local handicrafts. ⓐ Via Tavolara Eugenio ⓣ 079 23 01 01
ⓞ 09.30–13.00, 17.00–20.00 Mon–Fri, 09.30–13.00 Sat

EXCURSIONS

Caffè al Duomo £ Just a few strides from the cathedral, this is a convenient if simple pitstop serving coffees, ice creams and simple pastas. ⓐ Piazza Duomo 38 ⓛ 07.00–22.00 Tues–Sun

Caffè Italiano £ A typical Italian café where the barista will concoct your macchiato just as you like it. Outdoor seating on busy Via Roma lined with orange trees. ⓐ Via Roma 42 ⓛ 07.00–late Mon–Sat

Caffè Accademia £–££ A wine bar and café with a covered outdoor seating and a great evening vibe. ⓐ Via Torre Tonda 11 ⓣ 079 23 02 41 ⓛ 08.00–late Mon–Sat

AFTER DARK

Restaurants
Il Posto ££ This is a sound option for lunch and dinner with cheap pizzas, a variety of meat dishes and lots of pasta on the menu. ⓐ Via Costa Enrico 16 ⓣ 079 23 35 28 ⓛ 12.30–14.45, 19.45–22.30 Mon–Sat

Zia Forica ££ One of the most authentically Sardinian eateries in town with a menu featuring donkey and horse as well as a selection of less exotic staples. ⓐ Margherita di Savoia 39 ⓣ 079 99 42 628 ⓛ 12.00–1500, 19.00–late Mon–Sat

Oristano

A regional centre set 4 km (2½ miles) back from the arching Golfo di Oristano, the city of Oristano was founded around a millennium ago by people escaping Barbarian raids for the relative security of the hinterland.

Centred around a series of interconnecting piazzas, the city has an impressive cathedral and a sprinkling of undemanding sights as well as being a staging post for trips to the nearby ancient ruins at Tharros.

The best time of year to be in Oristano is February, during the **Sa Sartiglia** festival – an ancient masked horseback procession and jousting contest held at carnival time (see page 101).

THINGS TO SEE & DO

Corso Umberto and around

Corso Umberto, Oristano's main pedestrianised shopping precinct, runs north–south between two grand piazzas. To the south lies the **Piazza Eleanora d'Arborea**, filled on one side by the town hall, which gazes down on a statue of Eleanora d'Arborea (the Italian answer to Joan of Arc), famous for her stand against Spanish invaders in the 14th century. To the north extends the leafy **Piazza Roma** dominated by the **Torre di Mariano (Mariano Tower)**, dating from the 13th century and once the most prominent structure along the town's defensive walls. Those who venture to the top are rewarded with views across Oristano's red roofs and even the sea is visible when clear conditions prevail.
Mariano Tower ⓐ Piazza Roma ⓛ 10.00–12.00, 15.00–17.00 July & Aug

> **GETTING THERE**
> Located as it is on the north–south main line, Oristano is best reached from Cagliari and the northwest by train. There may also be the odd ARST bus from Bosa.

EXCURSIONS

Duomo di Santa Maria Assunta (Cathedral of Santa Maria Assunta)
Little remains of the original Gothic cathedral established here in the 13th century and the somewhat forlorn building we see today dates from the early 18th century. The octagonal almost free-standing bell tower is a 15th-century survivor and the cathedral's most impressive feature. The spacious interior is awash with baroque flourishes with the remnants of the Gothic original and various neoclassical and Renaissance touches thrown into the mix.
ⓐ Via Duomo 🕒 08.00–13.00, 16.00–19.00

Museo Archeologico Antiquarium Arborense (Archaeological Museum)
Housed in the Palazzo Parpaglia, former home of a 19th-century mayor of Oristano, this engaging archaeological museum boasts collections of Nuraghic, Carthaginian, Greek, Etruscan, Roman and medieval artefacts from the local area, and focuses in particular on nearby Tharros. There is also a gallery of medieval art on the first floor and some of the ground floor is given over to temporary exhibitions.
ⓐ Palazzo Parpaglia, Piazzetta Corrias ⓣ 078 37 91 262
ⓦ www.lamemoriastorica.it 🕒 09.00–14.00, 15.00–20.00 Mon, Wed & Fri–Sun (Sept–June), 09.00–14.00, 15.00–23.00 Tues & Thur (July & Aug) ❗ Admission charge

Tharros
Established by the Phoenicians in the 8th century BC on a spit of land, Tharros was a busy port throughout the Carthaginian and Roman period and was only completely abandoned in around AD 1000 when it came under attack from North African pirates. As in Nora on the southeast coast, much of what you see today dates from the Roman period with an aqueduct, temples and baths all clearly visible (using a little imagination). Much of the port areas on either side of the ruins lie submerged.

Atmospheric theatre performances take place here in the summer months. Ask at the information centre in Oristano for details.
ⓐ 15 km (9¼ miles) west of Oristano (near San Giovanni di Sinis)

ORISTANO

☎ 078 33 70 019 🌐 www.penisoladelsinis.it 🕑 09.00–sunset
ⓘ Admission charge. Reachable by public bus July & Aug only

TAKING A BREAK

For picnickers and self-caterers there's a handy Eurodrink supermarket located at Piazza Roma 21. Should you tire of pizza and horse steaks, Oristano, somewhat surprisingly, has a McDonald's.
ⓐ Via Cagliari 45

Azzurro £ In the heat of the early afternoon when the streets are devoid of life, the Azzurro is a welcome oasis of coffee, tasty Sardinian desserts and ice cream, which can be sampled indoors or out on the square at the foot of the Torre di Mariano. ⓐ Piazza Roma 73 ☎ 078 37 40 80 🕑 07.00–late

● *Piazza Eleanora d'Arborea*

EXCURSIONS

Bar Eleanora £ The most central café in town facing Eleanora's statue.
ⓐ Piazza Eleanora d'Arborea 1 ⓑ 07.00–23.00

AFTER DARK

Restaurants & bars

Bussu £–££ With 200 seats, a variety of dining spaces and a menu packed with Italian and traditional Sardinian dishes, such as *pecorino* cheese, Sardinian ham, roast lamb and suckling pig, this is one of the friendliest and busiest dinner spots in town. ⓐ Piazza Roma 54 ⓣ 078 37 37 61 ⓑ 07.30–02.00 Wed–Mon

La Bettola ££ The latest addition to Oristano's dining scene is only for those serious about delicious food prepared with top-quality local ingredients. A small shrine to Sardinian cooking, La Bettola has a different menu every day listing dishes such as rabbit, wild boar and *maloreddus alla campidanese* (pasta with sausage sauce), as well as the best island wines. ⓐ Vico Iosta 7 ⓣ 078 37 72 066 ⓑ 13.00–15.00, 20.00–23.00

Il Faro ££ Modern, kitsch-free eatery where the focus is firmly on tasty food – and here that means real Sardinian seafood dishes. For afters, be sure not to miss out on the *dolci Sardi* (Sardinian sweets). Located just to north of the centre, your taste buds will thank you for taking the walk. ⓐ Via Bellini 25 ⓣ 078 37 00 02 ⓑ 12.45–14.45, 20.00–22.00 Mon–Sat.

La Forchetta D'Oro ££ A recommended eatery though more for its top-notch food than its unlikely and unattractive setting amid a housing estate to the west of the historic centre. The limited menu features cheap pasta combinations, a selection of meat dishes (including horse steaks) and local wine. Excellent in its simplicity, but the ambience may put some off. ⓐ Via Giovanni XXIII 34 ⓣ 078 33 02 731 ⓑ 12.00–24.00

Iglesias

This former mining town, slightly off the beaten track in the far east of the island, is best known for its many churches from which it derives its name (*iglesia* is Spanish for church).

Despite its gritty past, it's a charming town with a mildly Spanish flavour and good for a half-day trip if spending an extended period on the island. Though light on eateries and shopping, Iglesias has an enchanting maze of old streets lined with tall town houses still sporting their Spanish-era wrought-iron balconies, some worthwhile churches and a long stretch of well-preserved Pisan-era defensive walls.

Visitors can also make the steep ascent to the **Chiesa del Buon Cammino** high up on a hill with sweeping views across the wide valley which the town occupies. A lot of EU funding is going into renovating run-down quarters in the town, which is keen to welcome tourists in the wake of the demise of its once-thriving industrial base.

Unless you want to stare at padlocks all day it's best to visit Iglesias on a weekday morning or evening.

THINGS TO SEE & DO

Churches

The obvious attractions in a town whose name translates as 'churches' are, not surprisingly, its churches. Pride of place goes to the **cathedral** with its bell tower of multicoloured stone dominating sloping Piazza del Municipio. The **Chiesa di San Francesco (Church of St Francis)** opposite the museum is a Gothic structure constructed in stages from the 14th to the 16th centuries. The nearby **Chiesa di Santa Maria delle Grazie (Church**

> **GETTING THERE**
> Sleek super-modern trains make the hour-long run from Cagliari and back. FS train C1 or C2 from Cagliari arrives at Via Garibaldi in Iglesias.

EXCURSIONS

◐ *Chiesa di Nostra Signora del Valverde*

of St Mary of Mercy) is wedged into the small square it occupies. Its façade is a curious mix of medieval base and almost tasteless baroque topping. The simple **Chiesa del Collegio (College Church)** on a square of the same name near the cathedral is predominantly baroque and once belonged to the Jesuits.

To the northwest of the historic centre, the **Chiesa del Buon Cammino (Church of the Good Way)** stands high on a steep hill. It will take fit visitors at least 15 minutes to ascend the asphalt road, which follows the **Vía Crucis (Stations of the Cross)**. The panoramic views from the church are a reward for the hard uphill slog, though the building itself is an unelaborate, modern affair. Another place of worship worth seeking out is the Gothic **Chiesa di Nostra Signora del Valverde (Church of Our Lady of Valverde)** behind the railway station.

Museo dell'Arte Mineraria (Mineral Museum)

This museum, housed in a former mining school, is more interesting than it may sound and worth half an hour's perusal (if open). There are displays of mining machinery, photographs and models. What's more, you can explore the tunnels beneath the building excavated by apprentices as part of their training. Upstairs you will find thousands of mineral specimens from the surrounding mines and quarries.

ⓐ Via Roma 9 ⓣ 078 13 50 037 ⓦ www.museoartemineraria.it
ⓛ 18.00–20.00 Sat & Sun (June); 18.30–20.30 Sat & Sun (July– Sept)

Piazza Sella

This leafy square laid out in the 19th century has a pleasant atmosphere and is an ideal place to unwind with a *gelato* or a picnic. Things get busy here in the evening when half the inhabitants of Iglesias, young and old, turn out in their Gucci and Armani gear to chew the fat and eye each other up.

Pisan walls

A long section of the town's defensive walls constructed by the Pisans in the 13th century has survived in Via Campidano on the way to the

EXCURSIONS

Chiesa del Buon Cammino. The turreted defences (4 m/13 ft high) interspersed with beefy watchtowers are currently undergoing renovation work.

TAKING A BREAK

Giardini Pubblici (Public Gardens) A wonderful old shady park to the south of the historic core with iron benches and a multitude of tree species. A fine picnic spot though you're not allowed on the grass. ⓐ Via V. Veneto

Chiosco Sella £ This outdoor café does a roaring trade under the varied foliage of the town's favourite square and rendezvous spot. ⓐ Piazza Sella ⓛ 07.00–late

Villa de Chiesa ££ Possibly Iglesias's best restaurant and bar. It has been serving food in the shadow of the cathedral on the main square for the past 43 years. The menu features all types of fare from traditional Sardinian to international staples, though the house speciality is seafood. The staff speak English and there is a reasonably priced tourist menu which includes house wine and water. ⓐ Piazza del Municipio 9/10 ⓣ 078 13 14 61 ⓛ 12.00–15.00, 19.00–24.00 (restaurant), 08.00–24.00 (bar)

AFTER DARK

Restaurant & bar
Gazebo Medioevale ££ A wonderful medieval tavern where you can feast on local specialities under bare-brick vaulting bedecked in bric-à-brac from days of yore. Portions are also fit for a medieval king and the service is first rate. ⓐ Via Musio 21 ⓣ 078 13 08 71 ⓦ www.gazebomedioevale.it ⓛ 12.00–15.00, 18.00–22.00

Nuraghe Santu Antine

A Nuraghe is a Bronze Age structure, typically built between 1600 and 600 BC, and unique to Sardinia. There are some 8,000 of these conical towers in various states of repair, though it is estimated 30,000 once pimpled the landscape. No one knows why the Nuraghic civilisation built them or what they were used for. Indeed, archaeologists have speculated for almost two centuries about their role as temples, lookout towers, palaces, tombs and astronomical observatories. These 20–25 m (66–82 ft) stone towers surrounded by dwellings were used until as late as the 2nd century BC when the Romans arrived. Their very survival to this day is testament to the skill of the Nuraghic builders. Wherever and however you travel around Sardinia, you will see them dotting farmers' fields across the land.

A large concentration of Nuraghi can be found in the Valle dei Nuraghi (Valley of the Nuraghe) about 30 km (18½ miles) east of Alghero. The biggest and best-preserved is the Nuraghe Santu Antine near the village of Torralba, a sliproad away from the S131 north–south motorway.

THINGS TO SEE & DO

Museo Comunale della Valle dei Nuraghe (Museum of the Valley of the Nuraghi) Located in the village of Torralba around 3 km (2 miles) to the north of Nuraghe Santu Antine, this museum was undergoing much-needed renovation at the time of writing. The new exhibition

GETTING THERE
Santu Antine and Torralba are easily reached by car from the island's main motorway. The scenic drive from Alghero can also form part of a day trip from the coast. Should you be lacking a set of wheels, Torralba lies on the main railway line between Cagliari and the north.

EXCURSIONS

⬤ *The remains of the Nuraghe Santu Antine*

NURAGHE SANTU ANTINE

promises to put more meat on the bones of the Nuraghic sites than the old one did.

ⓐ Via Carlo Felice 143 ⓣ 079 84 71 45 ⓦ www.nuraghesantuantine.it
❶ Ticket also valid for Nuraghe Santu Antine

Santu Antine

Built at the end of the 16th century BC, this is one of the best-preserved Nuraghi in Sardinia. The central tower, which was once 25 m/82 ft tall (17 m/56 ft remains), was tightly encircled by a village, the walls of which can be made out around the site. This Nuraghe is a very interactive, hands-on affair, and visitors can clamber over any part of the structure, crawl through any tunnel and peep through any window. Particularly impressive are the illuminated tunnels, which pass through the tower, and the view across the wheat fields of the Valle dei Nuraghi surrounded by high hills. The other large Nuraghe visible from Santu Antine across the valley floor is **Oes**, a less well-pruned tower which can be visited free of charge.

ⓐ 3 km (2 miles) south of Torralba ⓣ 079 84 71 45
ⓦ www.nuraghesantuantine.it (in Italian only) ⓛ 09.00–20.00
❶ Admission charge; tickets also valid for museum in Torralba

TAKING A BREAK

Bar Palmas £ This café and bar almost next door to the Museum of the Valley of the Nuraghi in Torralba serves drinks and sandwiches. ⓐ Via Nuoro 3 ⓛ 07.30–14.00, 16.00–23.00 Tues–Sun

Carlo Felice £ The cultural epicentre of Torralba is the Carlo Felice with a cinema upstairs and a fast food joint downstairs selling incredibly cheap pizzas, panini, desserts and drinks. ⓐ Via Carlo Felice 192 ⓛ 06.30–24.00

EXCURSIONS

La Maddalena Archipelago

This archipelago comprises seven islands (only three of which are inhabited) and lies just off the northern tip of Sardinia. La Maddalena, the largest town in the archipelago, lies on the largest island of the same name. It is reachable by regular car ferry from the mainland town of Palau.

The main attractions on offer are the ferry journey, the town's harbour-side seafood restaurants and bars, cycle or quad-bike trips to the neighbouring island of Caprera (where Garibaldi spent his retirement) and boat trips to some of the other outlying islands. Alternatively, you may just prefer to wander La Maddalena's charming old town, sip a cappuccino on Piazza Garibaldi, and watch the comings and goings in the busy harbour.

The entire archipelago and some neighbouring islets belonging to Corsica have enjoyed national park status since 1997.

BEACHES

The two main islands (La Maddalena and Caprera) have countless incredibly picturesque and secluded sandy coves, though you'll need your own transport to reach them.

THINGS TO SEE & DO

Chiesa di Santa Maddalena & Museo Diocesano Sacristia Santa Maria Maddalena (Church of St Mary Magdalene & Diocesan Museum of Religious Art)

To call the rather uninspiring neoclassical church of St Mary Magdalene the town's only tourist sight would be scraping the barrel. However, the Diocesan Museum of Religious Art, accessed from within the church, is of particular interest to British visitors. In addition to the interesting collection of gold and coral jewellery and other treasures dedicated as votive offerings to the church by townspeople, the first case by the door

LA MADDALENA ARCHIPELAGO

contains two silver candlesticks, a crucifix and a handwritten letter, all given to the church by Admiral Nelson. He used La Maddalena as a base when blockading Toulon in 1804, though allegedly never came ashore.

Diocesan Museum of Religious Art ⓐ Chiesa Parrocchiale S. Maria Maddalena, Via Ilva 1 ⓣ 078 97 37 400 ⓞ 10.00–12.00, 15.00–20.00 Tues–Sun ❶ Admission charge

Museo del Compendio Garibaldino (Museum of Garibaldi's Compendium)

Most non-Italians don't get further than the distractions of La Maddalena town. However, the neighbouring island of Caprera has great historic significance for Italians, because it was here, on the half of the island he personally owned, that Giuseppe Garibaldi spent the last 27 years of his life, writing and tending his farm. His house, the Casa Bianca, is now a museum and has pretty much been preserved as he left it. He is buried in the garden.

> ### GETTING THERE
> Getting to La Maddalena is half the fun, as it involves a 20-minute ferry journey from Palau on the mainland. Small boats operated by EneRmaR make the journey every 30 minutes in both directions from early morning until late at night when Saremar takes over.
>
> **EneRmaR** ⓣ 078 97 08 484 ⓦ www.enermar.it
> **Saremar** ⓣ 892 123 ⓦ www.saremar.it
>
> Getting to Caprera from La Maddalena is very straightforward. The two places are joined by a bridge making it possible to walk, cycle or ride across from La Maddalena. To make the journey, you can hire a bike, scooter or quad bike from Fratelli Cuccu or Vacanze.
> **Fratelli Cuccu** ⓐ Via Amendola 30 ⓣ 078 97 38 528
> **Vacanze** ⓐ Via Mazzini 1 ⓣ 078 97 35 200

EXCURSIONS

○ *Travel by ferry to La Maddalena*

LA MADDALENA ARCHIPELAGO

ⓐ Isola di Caprera ⓣ 078 97 27 162 ⓦ www.compendiogaribaldino.it
ⓛ 09.00–13.30 Tues–Sun ⓘ Admission charge except under-18s and over-65s

TAKING A BREAK

For picnickers and self-caterers there is a convenient Despar supermarket opposite the ferry landing.

Da Robys £–££ Nobody makes bigger and better pizzas than Da Robys. Pop in for a quick lunch or an evening takeaway and a friendly chat with the English-speaking pizza chef. ⓐ Via Amendola 2 ⓣ 078 97 37 727 ⓛ 10.30–23.00 (occasionally closed for one hour in the afternoon)

Gran Caffè Garibaldi £–££ The best place to sip a coffee or grab a bite to eat is bustling Piazza Garibaldi and the best place to do it is the Gran Caffè. The no-nonsense menu, service, opening hours and location mean it's well frequented by tourists and locals alike. ⓐ Piazza Garibaldi 8/9 ⓣ 078 97 37 003 ⓛ 06.00–late

Madrau Bar £–££ Not as good as the Gran Caffè across the flagstones of the piazza but its outdoor seating has the same busy atmosphere and is a sound option if its rival is full. ⓐ Piazza Garibaldi 2 ⓛ 07.00–late

AFTER DARK

The Penny Drops £ As seems to be the case with Sardinia's Celtic taverns, the Irishness stops at the sign above the door and the Guinness® on tap. This place is relatively convincing inside with lots of dark wood and a range of Irish beers on offer, but the panini and opening hours bring you right back to Italy. All in all, though, as good a watering hole as you'll find in northern Sardinia. ⓐ Piazza Santa Maria Maddalena
ⓣ 349 62 39 273 ⓛ 10.30–late July & Aug; 18.00–late Sept–June

EXCURSIONS

Enoteca Osteria Lio ££ This La Maddalena institution has been serving customers in some guise or other for 180 years! The friendly multilingual staff will serve you a summer menu of fish and pasta or a very reasonable tourist menu in the two cool dining spaces inside or outside behind the building. ⓐ Corso Vittorio Emanuele 4 ⓣ 078 97 37 507 ⓦ www.osterialio.com ⓛ 12.30–14.30, 20.00–23.00

La Grotta ££–£££ The Grotto lives up to its name, housed as it is in a cave-like ground-floor cellar. If you like seafood, you'll love this place with its daily menu of fresh and exclusively locally caught fish and *frutti di mare*. ⓐ Via Principe di Napoli 3 ⓣ 078 97 37 228 ⓦ www.lagrotta.it ⓛ 12.00–16.00, 19.00–24.00

Perla Blu ££–£££ This large, relatively upmarket pizzeria and restaurant on the harbour side is one of the archipelago's finest eateries with a tastebud-pleasing menu of pasta, pizzas, fish fresh from the boat and homemade tiramisu. The alfresco dining area has views of the harbour other restaurateurs in town can only leer at with envy. ⓐ Piazza Barone des Geneys ⓣ 078 97 35 373 ⓛ 12.30–15.00, 19.00–23.00

● *Typical street in Oristano*

LIFESTYLE
The Sardinian way

LIFESTYLE

Food & drink

Food is serious business in Sardinia, as it is across mainland Italy. The vast majority of Sardinians take great care about and pride in what they put on their plates and in their mouths. Only the tastiest, ripest, freshest ingredients will do, and most Sardinians (even those who don't cook) can elaborate for hours on the best ways to prepare dishes. Sardinian fare is similar to mainland food, though there are certain dishes, especially those found inland and away from the tourist resorts, which even visitors from Rome and Naples wouldn't recognise.

BREAD & CHEESE

Enter a bakery and you will be faced with a dizzying selection of bread. No other nation on earth produces so many different types of loaf and bun. Possibly the strangest is *pane carasau*, which is sometimes nicknamed *carta da musica* (music paper), thin crispy bread sold in 10 or 20 sheet-thick wheels. Choice on the cheese front is not as wide. Many will know Sardinia's signature cheese called *pecorino*, which is produced from ewe's milk, as is most *formaggio* on the island. *Pecorino* has a very strong taste and can be quite overwhelming for some. It is one of the main ingredients in pesto sauce and Sardinia produces three-quarters of all the *pecorino* consumed in Italy.

MEAT & SEAFOOD

Sardinia has some great seafood restaurants, but traditionally the locals eat meat. Not satisfied with beef, pork and chicken, they seem to have moved on to many other members of the animal kingdom, so don't be surprised to find some rather more exotic fare, including mutton, boar, horse, donkey and their various innards and appendages on the menu. The mysterious dark maroon meat on sale at the supermarket is horse. Lamb and suckling pig are also popular, as is goat, which can be a bit tough and stringy for some. Rabbit, partridge and veal also feature on some inland menus. Most resort restaurants stick to less exotic cuts of meat.

Eating out Sardinian style is an experience to be savoured

LIFESTYLE

The seafood tradition, even though not wholly native to Sardinia, has blossomed nonetheless. Tuna, lobster, mullet and sea bass are the dishes to try. Alternatively, you could go for *botarga*, which is mullet, swordfish or tuna roe, dried, cured and coated in beeswax then grated over pasta.

PASTA
Pasta is normally eaten as a starter and on menus you will find the usual Italian macaroni, penne, spaghetti and spirali coated in various tomato or cream-based sauces. Sardinia also has its own forms of pasta such as *malloreddus* (tiny shell-shaped pasta served with sauce or seafood) and *culurgiones* (a kind of Sardinian ravioli).

PIZZA
Pizza is the best and (arguably) the healthiest fast food around. There's nothing better than a thin-crusted disc of pastry daubed in tomato, cheese and a couple of delicious toppings. These range from mushrooms, ham and different types of cheese to seafood, anchovies and meatballs. For the amount per serving, pizzas are a cheap eat and ideal for family meals when they can be shared.

DESSERTS
A meal is not a meal in Sardinia if it is not rounded off with a dessert. Items you may find on the sweet trolley include ice cream, tiramisu, pastries, almond biscuits, crème caramel and *sebadas* (pastry filled with ricotta cheese then drizzled with honey). Sardinians are rightly proud of their fine flowery honey, which is often sold in souvenir shops.

VEGETARIANS
Despite all of Europe's domesticated animals featuring heavily in menus at some establishments, vegetarians don't do badly in Sardinia. Many pizzas and pasta dishes contain no meat, and if you are vegetarian of the fish-eating variety, then you're in luck. Soups such as minestrone or lentil are suitable and risotto is also an option.

DRINKS

After a meal of traditional fare, finish off with a bottle of Sardinian wine. The island produces dessert wines, strong reds, light whites and rosés. Wines to look out for are Cannonau (red), Vermentino (white), Torbato (white), Semidano (white) and Campidano di Terralba (red and white).

Wine is normally sold by the decanter (quarter, half-a-litre or litre) or by the bottle.

If you are familiar with spirits on the Italian mainland, you'll recognise *filu 'e ferru* as grappa. The odd name (which means iron wire) comes from a time when the state had a monopoly over the production of spirits. People would distil their own then bury the bottles so the authorities wouldn't find them, leaving only a wire sticking out of the ground to remind them where it was. *Mirto* is another indigenous firewater. It is made from myrtle leaves and comes in red and white varieties.

Ichnusa, Sardinia's favourite beer, is brewed in Assemini (near Cagliari) and is a very quaffable brew. International beers and ales from around Europe are also widely available.

Of course no one can leave Sardinia without trying Italian coffee. Cappuccinos, espressos, macchiatos and americanos are just as good here as in Milan or Rome and downed just as swiftly. Tea is best drunk iced in summer otherwise expect a stale tea bag and a cup or glass of tepid water.

LIFESTYLE

Menu decoder

Sadly, menus in English – even in tourist resorts – are rare. At some inland eateries menus even reject Italian, preferring instead to use the traditional Sardinian names, rendering the following menu decoder useless. However, Italian food is so international these days that deciphering menus tends not to be a huge problem. Occasionally you may come across a place with a 'verbal menu' (none listed in this guide).

MEALS AND COURSES
Prima colazione Breakfast
Pranzo Lunch
Cena Dinner
Antipasto Starter
Primi piatti First courses
Secondi piatti Second courses
Dolci Desserts

MEAT
Agnello Lamb
Asino Donkey
Capretto Kid
Cavallo Horse meat
Cinghiale Wild boar
Comiglio Rabbit
Fegato Liver
Maiale Pork
Manzo Beef
Montone Mutton
Monzette Snails
Pancetta Bacon
Pollo Chicken
Porcheddu Spit-roast suckling pig
Prosciutto Ham
Salsiccia Sausage
Trippa Tripe
Vitello Veal

SEAFOOD
Acciughe Anchovies
Aragosta Lobster
Arselle Clams
Baccalà Dried salted cod
Bottarga Poor man's caviar: mullet, swordfish or tuna roe dried, cured and coated in beeswax
Calamari Squid
Cozze Mussels
Gamberi Prawns
Granchio Crab
Ostriche Oysters
Polpo Octopus
Rospo Monkfish
Tonno Tuna

PASTA
Al dente Pasta which offers some resistance when

chewed – not overcooked in other words
Arrabbiata Sauce of tomato and chilli
Carbonara Sauce of egg, bacon and cream
Con pesto With pesto, a basil, pecorino and pine nut sauce
Culingiones Sardinian ravioli stuffed with *pecorino* cheese and spinach
Malloreddus Small shell-shaped pasta or gnocchi typical for Sardinia
Matriciana Sauce of tomato and bacon
Parmigiano Parmesan cheese
Ragù Meat sauce

PIZZA

All pizzas (except the Marinara) have a base of mozzarella and tomato passata. Those looking for pineapple chunks on the menu will be disappointed and considered insane should they request such. Onions are also rare.

Capricciosa With a combination of toppings, anything goes
Frutti di mare With seafood
Funghi With mushrooms
Margherita With tomato, mozzarella and oregano
Marinara With tomato and garlic
Napoletana With anchovies and olive oil
Quattro formaggi With four types of cheese
Quattro stagioni Divided into four sections with a different topping on each

DESSERTS

Amarettus Cakes made with almond flour
Aranciatte Sweets made with almonds, oranges and honey
Gelato Ice cream
Macedonia Fruit salad
Pardulas Cheese-filled pastries flavoured with vanilla and lemon
Sebadas A large circular pastry filled with ricotta cheese and soaked in honey

DRINKS

Acqua minerale Mineral water
Acqua normale Tap water
Bianco White
Birra Beer
Caffè Coffee
Cioccolata calda Cocoa
Con gas, frizzante Sparkling
Filu 'e ferru Sardinian grappa

LIFESTYLE

Latte Milk
Mirto Myrtle spirit
Rosso Red
Senza gas Still
Tè Tea
Vino Wine

OTHERS
Aglio Garlic
Formaggio Cheese
Insalata Salad
Miele Honey
Olio Oil
Pane Bread
Pane frattau Layers of thin bread with hot tomato sauce and grated *pecorino* cheese
Panna Cream
Pecorino A sharp-tasting ewe's cheese similar to Parmesan
Riso Rice
Risotto Rice cooked in stock and wine
Sale Salt
Zucchero Sugar
Zuppa Soup

⬤ *A typical bakery display including Sardinian pastries*

LIFESTYLE

Shopping

There is much to delight the shopaholic on this island, and if you are the type whose suitcase on departure weighs more than it did when you arrived, full as it is of local handicrafts and bottles of red, white, rosé and firewater, then you've come (or are intending to go) to the right place. Souvenirs and gifts are very easy to buy, with every third or fourth shop in some of the more frequented parts of the island seemingly a souvenir emporium. Some, such as Castelsardo's Mostra Mercato dell'Artigianato, have turned into huge retail outlets where they 'stack them high and sell them cheap'. Others, such as Alghero's Aradena and the ISOLA outlets, sell only authentic, locally produced items of the highest quality.

CORK & CERAMICS

Cork is one of the most common souvenirs. Stripped from the lower part of the trunk of the cork oak (the newly de-corked trees can be seen all over the island), it can be made into a whole host of items, not just the usual coasters and table mats. Cork is even used to coat bottles.

Alongside cork you are very likely to find traditional ceramics. Sardinia has a long tradition of ceramic production (as can be seen in the island's archaeological museums) and some of the items on sale are beautiful in their simplicity.

WICKERWORK

Wickerwork and baskets are produced on the doorsteps of Castelsardo and Bosa, and can often be bought direct from the maker. Reeds, willow, straw and dwarf palm fronds are all used to create simple but attractive household items.

CARPETS & TAPESTRIES

With all those sheep roaming the hills and mountains of the interior, it can come as no surprise that Sardinia produces exquisite woollen carpets and tapestries, arguably the best souvenir to take home. The coarse wool is often woven in ornate geometric patterns in every colour of the rainbow. The wool used to make authentic ISOLA-approved carpets is still dyed the traditional way using various flowers, bark, roots and minerals.

CORAL & SILVER

Many look on in horror at the sheer amount of coral Sardinians trawl up from the bottom of the surrounding seas to make jewellery to sell to tourists. However, this industry is strictly regulated and, it is claimed, all the coral is extracted from sustainable sources. The pink and turquoise jewellery made from coral can be stunningly beautiful, though watch out for cheap plastic imitations. Silver jewellery is also common, though traditional forms may not be to modern tastes.

KNIVES

Every Sardinian male worth his salt owns a knife and traditional shepherd's knives are produced on this island uniquely. The best are made to order by master craftsmen from the best steel and wood or

● *Making wickerwork*

horn for the handle into which the blade folds. A proper Sardinian knife should have a pointed blade resembling a myrtle leaf, though they come in all different shapes and sizes.

The best knives are produced in the villages of Santu Lussurgiu (southeast of Bosa) and Pattada (near Ozieri), though they are available in specialist shops all over the island (Aradena in Alghero has a good selection). If you buy one, just remember not to put it in your hand luggage for the flight home!

FASHION ITEMS
Away from the traditional, Italian fashions such as leather shoes, bags, purses and jackets are all available in Sardinia's larger towns and cities. Although slightly more expensive than on mainland Italy, prices may still be lower than back home.

> **ISOLA**
> ISOLA stands for Istituto Sardo Organizzazione Lavoro Artigiano. The task of this organisation is to promote and organise Sardinia's traditional craftsmen and the sale of their products (the acronym cleverly spells out 'island' in Italian). It protects the methods used in the production of traditional handicrafts and the symbols they display as well as guaranteeing quality and running special art and craft shops in four towns on the island (Cagliari, Sassari, Nuoro and Porto Cervo). These sell a wide range of ceramics, basketware, tapestries, carpets, timber furniture, jewellery and knives, which make fine souvenirs. Buying from ISOLA outlets as opposed to souvenir shops means you are making a direct contribution to the local rural economy and safeguarding the future of traditional craftsmanship on the island.
> Ⓦ www.regione.sardegna.it/isola

LIFESTYLE

Children

Sardinians just love children, so with little ones in tow you will feel welcome everywhere and even enjoy better service in many places. There is a family-friendly atmosphere wherever you go in Italy, and Sardinia is no exception.

The main attraction for children is the miles of glorious sandy beaches which they can play around on all day long. The beach usually provides sufficient entertainment, distraction and new friends to last the whole holiday.

When tummies begin to rumble, it's as if Italy's favourites, namely *gelato* and pizza, were thought up specially to satisfy wee taste buds. Restaurants often serve half portions for *bambini* and some even create special children's menus. Highchairs are part of the furniture in most decent eateries, though changing facilities in toilets are rare.

Away from the beach, Sardinia has few tourist sights or theme parks designed specifically with children in mind. The one exception to this is the **Mare Nostrum Aquarium** in Alghero (see page 39). However, inquisitive young minds will be fascinated by Sardinia's prehistoric Nuraghic sites, its illuminated caves, walled towns and castles.

As far as hazards for children in Sardinia are concerned, sunstroke is probably the greatest danger. To avoid this, keep your offspring in the shade during the hottest middle third of the day, make sure their heads are covered when in the sun and that they are not overheating while running around in playgrounds and the like. Make sure they drink plenty of fluids and are coated in a layer of sun block with an SPF of at least 15.

THE BIG SMOKE

Although Italy now has a smoking ban in public places, many Sardinians still light up half a metre from where they are no longer permitted to. This means smoky atmospheres still prevail in bus stations, railway terminals and the like, though the situation in bars and restaurants has improved immensely.

LIFESTYLE

🔽 *Snorkelling in the shallow waters is great fun for children*

The coastline also presents specific dangers with sea urchins waiting to be stepped on, and sharp rocks waiting to be fallen from/onto.

❶ Children under the age of 12 enjoy discounts on public transport and at tourist sights.
❶ Hotels may charge extra for putting a child's bed or cot in your room.
❶ Many of Sardinia's larger hotels now provide childminders and babysitters for an extra charge.

LIFESTYLE

Sports & activities

The island's wealth of coastline, mountains, valleys and caves means there is a wide variety of sport on offer in Sardinia. Watersports are the natural choice and every resort has several gear rental agencies, diving schools and qualified instructors. The best spots for diving are around the La Maddalena Archipelago, Capo Carbonara south of Villasimius and Capo Caccia in the northwest. Further out to sea, fishing trips run from almost every port.

The most popular inland activities are cycling and walking. The best hiking country is the rugged landscape around Nuoro where you can really feel you have escaped the clutches of civilisation. Hiking is one of the best ways to explore the interior and will allow you to reach places roads never will. However, marked trails are rare, so you'll need a good map and perhaps even a guide if you lack experience of the mountain environment. Anywhere in Sardinia is good for cycling, though in summer the traffic-choked roads are best avoided.

Sardinia has long been a favourite with rock climbers, who appreciate its wild, mountainous interior and dry summer weather. The principal climbing area can be found around the village of Cala Gonone on the east coast (W www.climb-europe.com/sardinia/cala-gonone.htm); other good locations include Isili, Domusnovas and Supramonte.

SPECTATOR SPORT

Cagliari football club (or the Rosoblu, as they are nicknamed) play in Italy's Serie A, entertaining sides such as Juventus, AC Milan and AS Roma on a regular basis. If you are into football, watching a match when one of the Italian giants is in town makes for an unmissable opportunity.

Cagliari Stadium a Viale la Playa t 070 60 42 01
W www.cagliaricalcio.net (in Italian)

LIFESTYLE

🔺 *Il Pevero golf course*

Sardinia has become a popular golf tourism destination in recent years and now boasts six golf clubs. The following are regarded as having the highest standard of courses and facilities.

Is Arenas Golf & Country Club, located on the west coast. ⓐ Pineta Is Arenas, Narbolia ⓣ 078 35 20 36 ⓦ www.isarenas.it
Is Molas An 18-hole course in the southeast of the island. ⓐ Santa Margherita di Pula ⓣ 070 92 41 006 ⓦ www.ismolas.it
Il Pevero Conceived by the Aga Khan himself, this coastal course is generally regarded as one of the most beautiful in the world.
ⓐ Porto Cervo, Località Cala di Volpe ⓣ 078 99 58 000
ⓦ www.golfclubpevero.com

LIFESTYLE

Festivals & events

It seems not a week goes by in Sardinia without a feast, festival or celebration somewhere on the island. Some events are specific to one location, some are nationwide affairs; most are religious occasions, often rooted firmly in a distant pagan past, but all of them are colourful experiences with much dressing up, eating, drinking and merrymaking. The following is a list of the main festivities, but there are many smaller annual events which take place in the scattered communities of inland Sardinia and around the coast.

🔺 *Amazing costumes at La Sagre del Redentore in Nuoro*

LIFESTYLE

FEBRUARY
Countrywide – Mardi Gras (Shrovetide Carnival)
Almost every community around Sardinia holds a carnival procession. While none match the flair and colour of Rio or Funchal, some events such as those in Nuoro have a dark local pagan flavour.
Oristano – Sa Sartiglia A full-blown medieval jousting tournament and horsemanship spectacular held since the arrival of the Spanish and part of the town's Carnival celebrations.

MARCH/APRIL
Countrywide – Easter Processions bearing Jesus on the cross take place across the country. One of the biggest events takes place in Iglesias where there are processions every day for a week.
Countrywide – Festa di Sant'Antioco (Festival of St Antiochus) Three days of music and feasting in honour of St Antiochus which begin on the second Sunday after Easter.

MAY
Cagliari & Nora – Festa di Sant'Efisio (Festival of St Ephisius) One of the largest festivities of the year celebrates the delivery of Cagliari from the plague by the martyr St Ephisius. A procession makes its way out of Cagliari and travels 40 km (25 miles) to Nora and the Chiesa di Sant'Efisio (Church of St Ephisius). The event is arguably Sardinia's most colourful.
Sassari – La Cavalcata Sarda (The Sardinian Ride) Another celebration featuring the island's feisty chargers and riders performing daring feats of horsemanship marks the defeat of Muslim invaders around the year 1000.

JULY
Sédilo – S'Ardia (Horse race) One of the most exciting celebrations on the island, which sees young locals hurtling around the Chiesa di Sant'Antine (Church of St Anthony) on horseback at breakneck speed. The race is held in honour of San Constantino (Roman emperor Constantine) and is not for the faint-hearted nor horse-lovers.

LIFESTYLE

> **PUBLIC HOLIDAYS**
> **New Year's Day** 1 January
> **Epiphany** 6 January
> **Easter Monday** March/April
> **Liberation Day** 25 April
> **Labour Day** 1 May
> **Anniversary of the Foundation of the Republic** 2 June
> **Feast of the Assumption** 15 August
> **All Saints' Day** 1 November
> **Feast of the Immaculate Conception** 8 December
> **Christmas Day** 25 December
> **St Stephen's Day** 26 December

AUGUST
Nuoro – La Sagre del Redentore (Festival of the Redeemer) One of the best opportunities to see the vibrant colours of inland Sardinia's folk costumes. The whole event is a kind of costume contest.

Sassari – I Candelieri (The Candlesticks) Huge wooden candles normally stored in the town's Chiesa di Santa Maria di Betlem (Church of St Mary of Bethlehem) are carried through the streets to celebrate the fact that Sassari was spared from the plague in the 15th century.

NOVEMBER
Countrywide – Tutti i Santi or Ognissanti (All Saints' Day) A big day across the Catholic world when families visit the graves of their relatives and feast in their honour.

DECEMBER
Countrywide – Natale (Christmas) Traditional Catholic yuletide events across the country. Nativity scenes are set up in churches and special masses, including midnight mass on 24 December, are held.

▶ *The busy Cagliari market*

PRACTICAL INFORMATION
Tips & advice

PRACTICAL INFORMATION

Accommodation

The price ratings below are based on the average cost of a double room in high season.

£ = up to €50   **££** = €50–€100   **£££** = over €100

ALGHERO

San Francesco ££ The 20-room San Francesco gives its guests the chance to stay in the heart of Alghero's historic centre where there are very few other options. The sometimes cramped rooms are situated in a 14th-century cloister, part of the Church of San Francesco.
ⓐ Via Ambrogio Machin ⓣ 079 98 03 30 ⓦ www.sanfrancescohotel.com
ⓔ info@sanfrancescohotel.com

BOSA

Sa Pischedda ££ Since 1896 the Sa Pischedda has been the last word in hotel accommodation in the centre of Bosa. With its stylish historic interiors, superb restaurant, pretty views and atmospheric rooms it is the obvious choice for anyone wanting to stay in the town. ⓐ Via Roma 8
ⓣ 0785 373 065 ⓦ www.hotelsapischedda.it

CAGLIARI

Albergo Aurora £–££ Located in the thick of the action on central Piazza Jenne, this is the best option for anyone on a budget. Rooms are simple and only some have en suite facilities. The price includes breakfast which is served at a small café across the street. ⓐ Piazza Jenne 19
ⓣ 070 65 86 25 ⓦ www.hotelcagliariaurora.it

Hotel Regina Margherita £££ This very comfortable 100-room, four-star establishment occupies a modern six-storey building in the centre of the old town, just east of the Marina District.
ⓐ Viale Regina Margherita 44 ⓣ 070 67 03 42
ⓦ www.hotelreginamargherita.com
ⓔ booking@hotelreginamargherita.com

PRACTICAL INFORMATION

CASTELSARDO
Hotel Nadir ££ On the road leading out of Castelsardo towards Lu Bagnu, this modern, reasonably priced hotel has all the facilities one would expect of a four-star establishment. ⓐ Via Colle di Frigiano 1 ⓣ 079 47 02 97 ⓦ www.hotelnadir.it

ORISTANO
Mariano IV Palace Hotel ££ Oristano's best hotel is conveniently situated just outside the historic centre and offers comfortable, excellent-value en suite accommodation. ⓐ Piazza Mariano 50 ⓣ 0783 360 101 ⓦ www.m4ph.eu

PORTO CERVO
Cervo Hotel £££ Excruciatingly expensive, the five-star Cervo is the place to see and be seen in this resort. The spacious, airy rooms are of the highest standard and the service and facilities are faultless. ⓐ Costa Smeralda, Porto Cervo ⓣ 0789 931 111 ⓦ www.starwoodhotels.com

PULA
Hotel Baia di Nora £££ You will find this four-star resort set just back from the Su Guventeddu beach near the Nora site. The spacious, well-furnished rooms are superb value and there's a great circular swimming pool in the grounds. ⓐ Strada Statale 195, Loc. Su Guventeddu ⓣ 070 92 45 551 ⓦ www.hotelbaiadinora.com

STINTINO
Silvestrino ££ A recently renovated three-star hotel in central Stintino. ⓐ Via Sassari 14 ⓣ 079 52 30 07 ⓦ www.hotelsilvestrino.it

VILLASIMIUS
Cormoran £££ Set just metres back from the waters of the Med, the Cormoran has all you need for a seaside holiday including two swimming pools, a restaurant, lots of sports facilities and comfortable rooms. ⓐ Località Campus ⓣ 070 79 340 ⓦ www.hotel-cormoran.com

PRACTICAL INFORMATION

Preparing to go

GETTING THERE
By plane
Sardinia is well served by budget and flag-carrier airlines. easyJet (W www.easyjet.com) operates flights from Luton to Cagliari and from Bristol and Gatwick to Olbia. Ryanair (W www.ryanair.com) flies from Birmingham to Olbia and Edinburgh and Bristol to Cagliari, and from Stansted, Liverpool and Dublin to Alghero. British Airways (W www.ba.com) has a service to Cagliari which also leaves from Gatwick amd BMI (W www.flybmi.com) shuttles between Alghero and East Midlands. A two-stage journey with Alitalia via Rome is a thing of the past and works out much more expensive than a direct flight. However, if you are arriving from outside Europe you will probably reach Sardinia via Rome, flying to Italy with Alitalia or your own country's airline and changing onto a flight to Cagliari.

Many people are aware that air travel emits CO_2, which contributes to climate change. You may be interested in the possibility of lessening the environmental impact of your flight through the charity Climate Care, which offsets your CO_2 by funding environmental projects around the world. Visit W www.jpmorganclimatecare.com

The following airlines fly to Sardinia:
BMI W www.flybmi.com
British Airways W www.ba.com
easyJet W www.easyjet.com
Ryanair W www.ryanair.com

Sardinia's airports
Alghero The two big cities of the northwest, Alghero and Sassari, officially share the region's airport which is, in fact, just outside the town of Fertilia W www.aeroportodialghero.it
Cagliari The capital's Elmas Airport is situated 6 km (4 miles) to the west of the city. W www.aeroportodicagliari.com
Olbia Costa Smeralda W www.geasar.it

PRACTICAL INFORMATION

By ferry
Having your own vehicle in Sardinia is a distinct benefit, and the only way to get your four-wheeled friend there is by boat. The main entry ports are Olbia and Porto Torres in the north, Arbatax on the east coast and Cagliari in the south.

> Ferries operate year-round on the following routes:
> Ajaccio–Porto Torres
> Bonifacio–Santa Teresa di Gallura
> Civitavecchia–Arbatax
> Civitavecchia–Cagliari
> Civitavecchia–Golfo Aranci
> Fiumicino–Arbatax
> Fiumicino–Olbia
> Genova–Olbia
> Genova–Porto Torres
> Livorno–Cagliari
> Livorno–Golfo Aranci
> Marseille–Porto Torres
> Napoli–Olbia
> Napoli–Palau
> Palermo–Cagliari
> Piombino–Golfo Aranci
> Porto Vecchio–Palau
> Propriano–Porto Torres
> Toulon–Porto Torres
> Trapani–Cagliari
> Tunis–Cagliari (via Trapani)

Ferry companies
CTN W www.ctn.com.tn
GNV W www.gnv.it
Grimaldi W www.grimaldi-ferries.com
MedMar W www.medmargroup.it
Moby W www.moby.it
SNAV W www.snav.it
SNCM W www.sncm.fr
Tirrenia W www.tirrenia.it

TOURISM AUTHORITY
With some notable exceptions (Alghero, Oristano, Pula and Cagliari), the provision of tourist information on Sardinia is poor to say the least. Locked doors, nonplussed staff, a dearth of English-speaking officials

PRACTICAL INFORMATION

○ *Street signs in Stintino*

PRACTICAL INFORMATION

and pointless brochures full of pretty pictures but little practical information are common features of most tourist offices on the island. If the office in a destination is closed or useless, try local travel agencies, which quite often double up as official or unofficial information points. Failing that you could seek out the local library, a bookshop or an upmarket hotel.

Tourist offices
Alghero @ Piazza Porta Terra 9 ❶ 079 97 90 54
Ⓦ www.comune.alghero.ss.it ℮ ufficioturismo@comune.alghero.ss.it
Bosa @ Via Azuni 5 ❶ 078 53 76 107 Ⓦ www.infobosa.it
℮ locobosa@tiscali.it
Cagliari @ Piazza Matteotti 9 ❶ 070 66 92 55
Ⓦ www.provincia.cagliari.it ℮ infoturismo@provincia.cagliari.it
Castelsardo @ Piazza del Popolo ❶ 079 47 15 06
Oristano @ Piazza Eleanora d'Arborea 19 ❶ 078 33 68 32 19
Ⓦ www.provincia.or.it ℮ enturismo.oristano@tiscalinet.it
Pula @ Casa Frau ❶ 070 92 09 264
Sassari @ Via Roma 62 ❶ 079 23 17 77

Australia @ Level 4, 46 Market Street, Sydney NSW 2000 ❶ 02 9262 1666
Ⓦ www.italiantourism.com.au ❶ 09.00–17.00 Mon–Fri
Canada @ 175 Bloor Street, East Suite 907, South Tower, Toronto M4W 3R8
❶ 416 925 4882 Ⓦ www.italiantourism.com ❶ 09.00–17.00 Mon–Fri
UK @ 1 Princes Street, London, W1B 2AY ❶ 020 7408 1254
Ⓦ www.italiantouristboard.co.uk ❶ 09.00–17.00 Mon–Fri
USA, Los Angeles @ 12400 Wilshire Boulevard, Suite 550, CA 90025
❶ 310 820 1898 Ⓦ www.italiantourism.com ❶ 09.00–17.00 Mon–Fri
USA, New York @ 630 Fifth Avenue, Suite 1565, NY 10111 ❶ 212 245 5618
Ⓦ www.italiantourism.com ❶ 09.00–17.00 Mon–Fri

BEFORE YOU LEAVE
No inoculations are necessary or recommended for visiting Sardinia. When packing, make sure to take a good sun cream or spray (factor 15

PRACTICAL INFORMATION

and over), sunglasses, a hat and light cotton clothing. Otherwise, almost anything you forget at home can be sourced in the island's main cities.

ENTRY FORMALITIES

Italy is a fully fledged member of the EU and party to the Schengen Agreement meaning that, by default, Sardinia is too – all good news for most travellers from Europe. If you are coming from another Schengen Zone country, you won't even have to show ID. UK visitors still need to produce a valid passport, as do those arriving from outside the EU (though the vast majority of flights to Sardinia originate in the EU). Should you need a visa to enter the EU or the Schengen Zone, contact your nearest Italian embassy or consulate.

MONEY

Sardinia is a relatively cheap province of a traditionally expensive country. Expect to pay less than you would in Britain for public transport, restaurant and supermarket food, coffee and cakes in cafés and admission to tourist sights, but more for clothes and luxury goods. Italy is part of the euro zone, which has led to price rises over the past decade.

Currency

Sardinia uses the euro (€) (or *francu* in Sardinian). Euro note denominations are 500, 200, 100, 50, 20, 10 and 5. Coins are 1 and 2 euros and 1, 2, 5, 10, 20 and 50 cents.

Cash machines

ATMs or cash machines are widespread and can be found in even the remotest of settlements. The vast majority accept all major cards, and instructions can almost always be accessed in English.

Credit cards and cheques

Use of plastic as a method of payment is widespread, and the vast majority of hotels and even campsites will accept cards. Away from your hotel lobby, many restaurants, shops, tour operators and tourist

PRACTICAL INFORMATION

A narrow street in picturesque Castelsardo

PRACTICAL INFORMATION

attractions around the island will accept them. If card payment is not an option, there'll almost always be a cash machine nearby where you can withdraw the required sum. Cards are not accepted when buying bus and train tickets, at the majority of small cafés and bars, and at markets. In this age of ATMs and electronic transactions traveller's cheques are becoming a waste of time and effort for the security they provide.

Tax
If you have bought an item on Sardinia worth more than the rather odd sum of €154.94 in one shop in one day, and you are flying out of the EU, you are eligible for a VAT refund. Visit the Global Refund website (w www.globalrefund.com) to learn about the various ways this can be done, and don't forget to keep all receipts, etc.

CLIMATE
Coastal resorts enjoy temperatures of around 28–32°C (86–90°F) in summer and around 15–20°C (68°F) in winter. Inland conditions can be more extreme with summer temperatures hitting 35°C (95°F) and winter temperatures approaching freezing. Most rain falls in the winter, though electric storms can bring heavy downpours in the heat-charged summer months. There is generally less rain in the south than in the north.

TRAVEL INSURANCE
However you arrange your holiday to Sardinia, it is important to take out adequate personal travel insurance for the trip. The policy you choose should provide cover for medical expenses, loss, theft, repatriation, personal liability and expenses incurred due to cancellations. Single trip insurance can now be purchased for just a few pounds or dollars but always read the small print to ensure the policy covers any activities you intend to do on the island such as mountain hiking and watersports.

PRACTICAL INFORMATION

BAGGAGE ALLOWANCE

As baggage allowances vary between airlines, the best idea is to check your airline or tour operator's website in advance, give them a call or check with your travel agent. Scheduled airlines usually offer higher baggage allowances than package-tour operators. British Airways currently allows economy-class passengers a single piece of luggage weighing 23 kg (nearly 51 lbs) to be stored in the hold and one piece of hand luggage, measuring 56 x 45 x 25 cm (approx 22 x 18 x 10 in), which must fit easily into overhead lockers. This includes women's handbags, but laptop computers can be taken on board in addition to your hand luggage. On British Airways flights there are hefty surcharges for checking in more than one main suitcase. easyJet allows one piece of hand luggage measuring 55 x 40 x 20 cm (approx 22 x 16 x 8 in) and one piece of checked luggage weighing up to 20 kg (44 lbs), with a fee for every kilogram over this weight. Ryanair levies a charge for all checked baggage and for every kilogram (2.2 lbs) over a 15-kg (33-lb) weight limit. Hand baggage must not weigh more than 10 kg (22 lbs) and be less than 55 x 40 x 20 cm in size.

🔺 *Alghero harbour*

PRACTICAL INFORMATION

During your stay

AIRPORTS
Alghero
Having collected your suitcases and cleared passport control and customs, the quickest way into town is by taxi (€20–€25). Local bus AA only runs to coincide with arrivals and departures, so if you miss it, you could have a long wait for the next one (tickets from a tiny inconspicuous machine next to the café in arrivals).

Cagliari
The city centre is well connected with Elmas Airport with almost two buses an hour leaving for Piazza Matteotti. A taxi will cost €15–€20.

COMMUNICATIONS
Phones
Public telephones can be found in all major settlements across Sardinia. Most of these only work with cards, which can be bought from tobacconists and news kiosks. Italy uses the GSM system, meaning mobile handsets from the UK and other countries in Europe will work the same as they do at home. Recent changes to tariffs in the EU mean it is now much cheaper to phone home (or anywhere in the EU) from your mobile. Mobiles from the USA and Canada may not work in Europe, and Australian and New Zealand handsets might need a change of band frequency.

Post
Italy's postal system (Poste Italiane ⓦ www.poste.it) does not have the best of reputations and rightly so. Your postcards will rarely make it to their destinations before you return from holiday and items going astray is still a lamentably common problem. Stamps can be bought from tobacconists, which is just as well, as tracking down an (open) post office anywhere in Italy is a feat in itself.

PRACTICAL INFORMATION

> **TELEPHONING ABROAD**
> All except mobile numbers on Sardinia start with 07 followed by seven or eight digits. The area code (the first three or four digits) must be dialled at all times. When calling from abroad, dial +39, the international code for Italy, then the full subscriber number. When calling abroad from Sardinia, dial 00 then your country code plus the subscriber number.
>
> **DIALLING CODES FROM ITALY**
> Australia **0061**
> New Zealand **0064**
> Republic of Ireland **0353**
> South Africa **0027**
> UK **0044**
> USA & Canada **001**

Internet

Internet cafés are not common around Sardinia and tend to be on the expensive side. In some resorts more popular with northern Europeans, ex-pats have started up a few convenient internet rooms. As far as WiFi is concerned, Sardinia is not yet quite a hotspot and this service is only available at top hotels. The Italian internet suffix is .it

CUSTOMS

With the possible exception of the Spanish-influenced northeast, most of Sardinia is a conservative and rather reserved place and Sardinians in general tend to be much less frenetic and intrusive than in mainland Italy. However, once you get to know them, you will find they are just as friendly and hospitable towards strangers, if not more so, than in Italy proper. Many visitors to Sardinia come away with the impression that the locals are some of the friendliest they have met but it does take some effort to break the ice. Sardinians tend to be very family-oriented and not only for economic reasons as some might suggest. They like

PRACTICAL INFORMATION

nothing more than to enjoy the company of friends and family over a good meal, on the beach, while strolling in the cool evening air or at a local festival or celebration. They are also very proud of their traditions and love to tell visitors about locally produced items and customs associated with the many religious festivals held on the island.

DRESS CODES

The only occasion visitors need to take heed of their attire is when visiting churches. Women should cover their heads, and short skirts, skimpy shorts and revealing tops are a definite no-no. Men should remove their hats, and shorts are frowned on but tolerated. If there is someone around inside the church when you visit, you *will* be asked to leave if you do not comply with the above.

ELECTRICITY

Sardinia works on 220 V AC, 50 Hz. To use electrical appliances from home you will need a Continental two-pin adaptor. Laptops from the USA using only 110 volts will need a transformer.

EMERGENCIES
Embassies & consulates
UK British Honorary Consul ⓐ Viale Colombo 160, Quartu Sant'Elena, Cagliari ⓣ 070 82 86 28 ⓔ britcon.cagliari@tiscali.it
US Embassy ⓐ Via Vittorio Veneto, 119/A, Rome ⓣ 06 467 41 ⓦ http://rome.usembassy.gov

> ### EMERGENCIES
> General EU emergency number ⓣ 112
> Ambulance ⓣ 118
> Coastguard ⓣ 1530
> Fire brigade ⓣ 115
> Police ⓣ 113
> Roadside assistance ⓣ 116

PRACTICAL INFORMATION

GETTING AROUND
Car hire
With limited public transport on the island, having your own set of wheels is a considerable advantage should you wish to strike out into the wilds of Sardinia's interior or even just make a day trip from one town to another. Roads are of a fairly good standard but most are narrow and winding. Stretches of fast road link Cagliari with Porto Torres (S131), Olbia with Abbasanta (S131DCN) and Cagliari with Iglesias (S130). It is best to stick to international car hire companies in Sardinia, as vehicles belonging to local firms can sometimes leave a lot to be desired.

● *The narrow-gauge* trenino verde *between Alghero and Sassari*

PRACTICAL INFORMATION

Alghero
Avis ⓐ Airport arrivals hall ⓣ 079 93 50 64 ⓐ Piazza Sulis 9
ⓣ 079 97 95 77 ⓦ www.avisautonoleggio.it
Hertz ⓐ Airport arrivals hall ⓣ 079 93 50 54 ⓦ www.hertz.it
Sixt ⓐ Airport arrivals hall ⓣ 079 93 60 46 ⓦ www.sixt.it

Cagliari
Avis ⓐ Elmas Airport arrivals hall ⓣ 070 24 00 81 ⓐ Via Roma
ⓣ 070 67 49 03 ⓦ www.avisautonoleggio.it
Hertz ⓐ Elmas Airport arrivals hall ⓣ 070 24 00 37 ⓐ Piazza Matteotti
ⓣ 070 65 10 78 ⓦ www.hertz.it
Sixt ⓐ Elmas Airport arrivals hall ⓣ 347 30 95 890 ⓦ www.sixt.it

Public transport
Bus Bus travel can be a frustrating experience in Sardinia and, as a rule, if there's a train, use it – forget the bus. Unfortunately, in many areas you will have no choice but to take the coach if relying on public transport. Infrequent services, tortuous detours off main roads, dirty graffiti-coated

> ### DRIVING RULES & CONDITIONS
> When driving in Sardinia you should:
> - drive on the right
> - keep to the speed limits (50 kph/31 mph in town, 90 kph/56 mph out of town, 120 kph/75 mph on the southern motorway)
> - use dipped headlights during the day
> - make sure your brakes and tyres are in good condition at all times
> - ensure all passengers are wearing a seatbelt
> - make sure children under 1.5 m (5ft) tall or under three years of age sit in the rear seats
> - avoid consuming alcohol before driving
> - carry a red warning triangle in the boot

PRACTICAL INFORMATION

coaches with dodgy clutches, grouchy drivers, an absolute lack of information at all but the largest stations and crumbling termini are just some of the pleasures of taking to the intercity bus network. Relatively inexpensive tickets are the traveller's sole consolation.

As throughout Italy, intercity coaches are blue. All tickets must be bought in advance and stamped in a machine behind the driver. Sourcing tickets for intercity coaches can be a pain as they are not often sold at the station but in a nearby café or bar. However, don't be afraid to board without a ticket in remote areas, as the driver will normally stop at the next 'sales point' to let you buy one.

The following companies operate coach services in various parts of the island.
ARST w www.arst.sardegna.it
FdS w www.ferroviesardegna.it
FMS w www.ferroviemeridionalisarde.it

City buses tend to be of a better standard, especially in Cagliari where the bus fleet is new and services regular. Suburban buses sport a yellowy-orange livery and, again, all tickets must be acquired prior to boarding from news kiosks and ticket offices.
Cagliari City Transport (CTM) w www.ctmcagliari.it

Train Rail services link large towns along a north–south axis running from Cagliari in the south to Porto Torres and Olbia in the north via Oristano and Sassari. There are also branch lines which run from: Cagliari to Iglesias; Cagliari to Mandas; Macomer to Nuoro; Olbia to Golfo Aranci; and Sassari to Alghero. Trains ply these lines year round, but in summer they are joined by the narrow-gauge *trenino verde* (little green train) services operated by FdS, which run between Arbatax and Mandas, Isili and Sorgono, Macomer and Bosa, and Sassari and Palau. These are tourist specials, though locals who are not in any hurry to arrive at their destination also use them. They are sometimes pulled by steam locomotives and with their winding routes through sometimes mountainous terrain constitute a relaxing way to see bits of the Sardinian countryside most wouldn't ordinarily reach.

There are no high-speed trains on the island with all services classed as *regionale* by Italian railways. This means trains stop at every station along the way, making for long journey times. All tickets must be bought in advance and stamped in ticket machines before boarding (except on the Sassari–Alghero route operated by FdS where they are inspected on board). Riding the rails is an inexpensive way of getting around and a preferable alternative to Sardinia's bus network.

FdS Ⓦ www.ferroviesardegna.it Ⓦ www.treninoverde.com
Trenitalia Ⓦ www.ferroviedellostato.it

By air

Olbia and Cagliari are linked by the island's only internal flight. This is operated daily except Tuesday by Meridiana and Edelweiss Air. Flights leave Olbia in the morning and return in the evening. The flight time is just over half an hour.

HEALTH, SAFETY & CRIME

Sardinia is generally a very safe place to holiday, though there are certain issues visitors should be aware of. With many holidaymakers renting cars on the island, traffic accidents are perhaps the greatest danger. Sardinian drivers are not as bad as their insane mainland cousins, but abysmal behaviour on the roads and poor car maintenance are all too common. If renting from a small local agency, check the state of the car before you drive away (especially the tyres and brakes).

If you are from the EU and encounter health problems or injury, your EHIC (European Health Insurance Card) entitles you to receive emergency treatment free of charge at any hospital. Non-EU nationals should make sure they take out adequate health insurance before travelling.

As far as criminality is concerned, petty theft, and in particular theft from rental cars, should probably be your main concern. Hide all valuables out of sight or take them out of your car altogether. Try to park

PRACTICAL INFORMATION

your car overnight in a secure parking facility where possible. Bag snatching from mopeds seems to have gone out of fashion slightly, but cases do still occur. Other than the odd camera disappearing from a restaurant table or a wallet being pilfered from a back pocket, crime against tourists is relatively rare. All crimes should be reported to the police, who will draw up a report for your insurance company should you need one.

LANGUAGE

Making yourself understood if you don't speak Italian can be problematic to say the least. The standard of foreign language knowledge in Sardinia (and the rest of Italy) is very poor and Italians even trail far behind traditional linguistic basket cases such as the British and French. Don't be surprised if waiters can't understand their own menu in English (or numbers), if hotel reception staff can't comprehend what the word 'room' means or a ticket seller at an attraction hasn't a clue what you mean by 'two tickets, please' – it really is that bad. Learning 100 words of Italian before you leave will solve 101 problems when you're there and is strongly advised. Menus in Sardinia are almost never in English and only the minimum of info in museums and other tourist sights will be in any other language than *Italiano*. The resort of Alghero is a shining exception to all the above with most people working in the tourist industry possessing a smattering of English.

Away from the linguistic barrier between tourist and local, Sardinia is a relatively interesting island when it comes to language. Although the vast majority of its inhabitants use Italian in everyday life, they may also be speakers of Sardinian, a tongue which bears a resemblance to ancient Latin. Elderly Algheresi also speak a form of Catalan.

MEDIA

There are no English language newspapers or 'what's on' type of magazines for tourists in Sardinia (perhaps someone should launch one). British and US newspapers can be found in Cagliari and other big cities one or two days after they are published. The biggest local

PRACTICAL INFORMATION

newspapers are *L'Unione Sarda* and *La Nuova Sardegna*, and the big Italian dailies are also available. Italian TV is virtually unwatchable and radio stations seem to pump out tinny copycat Italian pop interspersed with the odd track from Britain or the USA. Take a good book and your MP3 player.

OPENING HOURS

'Oh, it's closed' can be heard on the lips of many an irate tourist in Sardinia (and across Italy for that matter). *Chiuso* (closed) is among the first Italian words any tourist learns during a stay in Italy. Some restaurants open so few hours a week you wonder why the owners bother at all.

The opening times in this guide should be taken as a very rough guide. If the listing states that an eatery is open until 15.00, don't be surprised to find doors bolted and no sign of life whatsoever at 14.30. Restaurateurs will hold their kitchens open as long as there are paying customers at tables, but when the restaurant empties, they

○ *Ask at the tourist office if you need advice*

PRACTICAL INFORMATION

bang the doors shut as swiftly as possible and shoot off for a hard-earned siesta.

Restaurant staff will also helpfully inform you that 'the restaurant is open but the kitchen is closed', and don't be too surprised when a pizzeria only serves pizza at certain times of the day!

Visitors from 24-hour consumer societies just have to accept that in this part of the world the day is organised in a very different way. Unlike in Spain, the siesta is here to stay – despite all the trouble it causes mothers, workers and schoolchildren, not to mention the poor tourist.

Attractions 🕒 roughly 10.00–13.00 & 15.00–17.00; later in summer
Banks 🕒 08.30–13.30 & 15.00–17.00 Mon–Fri
Office hours 🕒 09.00–13.00 & 15.00–19.00 Mon–Fri
Shops 🕒 09.00–13.00 & 16.00–20.00 Mon–Sat; extended to 23.00 in summer

RELIGION

Italy is overwhelmingly Roman Catholic and Sardinia is no different. Churches across the island still fill up for mass at all times of the week, though congregations are nothing like as large as 50 years ago. The importance of the Church in Sardinia can be seen during the many colourful religious festivals and pilgrimages held throughout the year.

TIME DIFFERENCES

Sardinia is in a time zone one hour ahead of Greenwich Mean Time in winter and two hours ahead in summer. The clocks go forward one hour for daylight saving in March, and back again in October.

TIPPING

Most restaurant bills include a service or cover charge. If not, and you are satisfied with the food and service, leave around 10 per cent. Tipping is not common in small bars, cafés and cheap pizzerie, though leaving a few cents is always appreciated. Taxi drivers do not expect a tip.

PRACTICAL INFORMATION

TOILETS

It must be said that Sardinia doesn't do public conveniences very well. Stand-alone public toilets are almost non-existent, forcing visitors to utilise facilities in stations, cafés and bars. These can almost always be used free of charge, and, thankfully, proprietors normally don't mind non-guests in their loos. Standards range from new spick-and-span EU-funded conveniences with a list of times recording when the place was last checked by a cleaner, to stinking holes with squat toilets and no running water.

Confusion often arises when it comes to the signs on toilet doors. *Signori* means 'Gentlemen' and *Signore* means 'Ladies'. Make sure you get it right!

TRAVELLERS WITH DISABILITIES

Sardinia is not the worst country in Europe for travellers with mobility problems but there are issues disabled tourists should be aware of. While some hotels, restaurants and tourist sights have invested in ramps and lifts, many haven't. Buses are almost impossible to use, though trains can accommodate wheelchair users and railway stations tend to be more wheelchair-friendly than the island's crumbling bus termini. The nature of many Sardinian towns with their cobbled streets, steep hills and anarchic parking culture means there is always some obstacle or another to negotiate. Disabled toilets are rare. Tourist-savvy Alghero sticks out as possibly the best resort for people with disabilities.

The following organisations can offer advice and assistance to travellers with disabilities:

Access Travel ⓐ 6 The Hillock, Astley, Lancs M29 7GW ⓣ 01942 888844 ⓦ www.access-travel.co.uk
Holiday Care Services ⓐ The Hawkins Suite, Enham Place, Andover SP11 6JS ⓣ 0845 124 9971 ⓦ www.holidaycare.org.uk
SATH (Society for the Advancement of Travelers with Handicaps) ⓐ 347 5th Avenue, New York, NY 10016, USA ⓣ 212 447 7284 ⓦ www.sath.org

INDEX

A

accommodation 104–5
air travel 106, 114, 120
Alghero 37–45
Anfiteatro Romano 16
architecture 17–18, 33, 39, 56, 64, 66, 70, 73, 75
Asinara 47, 48

B

baggage allowances 113
Bastione San Remy 17
beaches 15–16, 25, 37, 47, 51, 55, 59, 80, 96
boats 48, 81, 107
Bosa 31–6
buses 21, 118–19

C

Cagliari 15–24
car hire *see* driving
Castello (Cagliari) 17
Castello Malaspina 31–2
Castelsardo 51–4
children 41, 96–7
churches and cathedrals 73–5
    Cattedrale di Santa Maria 17
    Chiesa del Buon Cammino 73, 75
    Chiesa di San Giovanni Battista 25
    Chiesa di Sant'Anna 18
    Chiesa di Sant'Efisio 25, 27
    Chiesa di Santa Maria 51
    Chiesa di Santa Maria di Betlem 64
    Chiesa di Stella Maris 56
    Duomo (Alghero) 39
    Duomo (Bosa) 33
    Duomo (Castelsardo) 52
    Duomo di San Nicola 64, 66
    Duomo di Santa Maria Assunta 70
climate 112
Costa Smeralda 55
crime 120–1
cycling 98

D

disabilities, travellers with 124
diving 47
driving 35, 77, 117–18, 120–1

E

emergencies 116
entry formalities 110
events 25, 27, 29, 69, 100–2

F

ferries *see* boats
food and drink 86–92
    eating out 96, 122–3 *see also individual resorts*
    filu 'e ferru 89
    menus 90–2
    pecorino 86
football 98
Fortezza Vecchia (Villasimius) 59

G

gardens and parks 20, 43, 48, 67, 76
golf 99
Grotta di Nettuno 43

H

health 96–7, 109–10, 120
hiking 98

I

Iglesias 73–6
insurance 112, 120
internet 115

L

La Maddalena Archipelago 80–4
language 121
Lu Bagnu 51

INDEX

M
Mare Nostrum Aquarium 39
media 121–2
money 110, 112
museums and galleries
    Casa Deriu 31
    Collezione di Cere Anatomiche 18, 20
    Museo Archeologico (Pula) 27
    Museo Archeologico (Villasimius) 59–60
    Museo Archeologico Antiquarium Arborense 70
    Museo Archeologico Nazionale (Cagliari) 18
    Museo d'Arte Siamese 18
    Museo del Compendio Garibaldino 81, 83
    Museo Comunale della Valle dei Nuraghi 77, 79
    Museo Diocesano d'Arte Sacra 39
    Museo Diocesano Sacristia Santa Maria Maddalena 80–1
    Museo dell'Intreccio Mediterraneo 52
    Museo Mineralogico Sardo 75
    Museo Nazionale Archeologico Etnografico 'G.A. Sanna' 66–7
    Museo della Tonnara 48
    Museo Virtuale 40
    Pinacoteca Nazionale (Cagliari) 18

N
nightlife 23–4, 30, 36, 44–5, 49, 54, 57, 60, 62, 68, 72, 76, 83–4
Nora 25, 27, 29
Nuraghi 41, 77–9

O
opening hours 122–3
Oristano 69–70, 71–2

P
Palazzo Giordano 67
Palazzo della Provincia (Sassari) 67
Palmavera 41
Pelosa, La 47
phones 114, 115
Poetto 15–16
Porto Cervo 55–7
post 114
Pula 25, 27, 29–30

R
religion 100–2, 123
rock climbing 98

S
safety 96–7, 118, 120–1
Santu Antine 79
Sassari 64–8
shopping 20, 33, 41, 52, 67, 93–5, 112
    cork 93
    ISOLA 20, 55, 67, 95
    knives 94–5
    wickerwork 93
smoking 96
Stintino 47–9

T
tax 112
Tharros 70–1
time differences 123
tipping 123
toilets 124
Torre dell'Elefante 21
Torre di Mariano 69
Torre di San Pancrazio 21
tourist information 107, 109
trains 33, 35, 41, 43, 66, 73, 119–20

V
Villasimius 59–62

ACKNOWLEDGEMENTS

ACKNOWLEDGEMENTS

The publishers would like to thank the following individuals and organisations for providing their photographs for this book, to whom the copyright belongs:

Paulo Curto/Tips Images page 99; Fototeca ESIT page 94; Mark Howland/BigStockPhoto.com page 5; Elisa Locci/BigStockPhoto.com page 42; Matteo Natale/BigStockPhoto.com page 8; Pictures Colour Library pages 10–11, 61, 103; World Pictures/Photoshot pages 53, 63, 100, 113; all the rest Marc Di Duca

Project editor: Penny Isaac
Layout: Donna Pedley
Proofreader: Lucilla Watson
Indexer: Karolin Thomas

Send your thoughts to
books@thomascook.com

- Found a beach bar, peaceful stretch of sand or must-see sight that we don't feature?
- Like to tip us off about any information that needs a little updating?
- Want to tell us what you love about this handy little guidebook and more importantly how we can make it even handier?

Then here's your chance to tell all! Send us ideas, discoveries and recommendations today and then look out for your valuable input in the next edition of this title.

Send an email to the above address or write to:
pocket guides Series Editor, Thomas Cook Publishing,
Thomas Cook Business Park, PO Box 227, Coningsby Road,
Peterborough PE3 8SB, UK

Useful phrases

English	Italian	Approx pronunciation
BASICS		
Yes	Sì	*See*
No	No	*Noh*
Please	Per favore	*Pehr fahvohreh*
Thank you	Grazie	*Grahtsyeh*
Hello	Buongiorno/Ciao	*Bwonjohrnoh/Chow*
Goodbye	Arrivederci/Ciao	*Ahreevehderchee/Chow*
Excuse me	Scusi	*Skoozee*
Sorry	Mi dispiace	*Mee deespyahcheh*
That's okay	Va bene	*Vah behneh*
I don't speak Italian	Non parlo italiano	*Non pahrloh eetahlyahnoh*
Do you speak English?	Parla inglese?	*Pahrlah eenglehzeh?*
Good morning	Buongiorno	*Bwonjohrnoh*
Good afternoon	Buon pomeriggio	*Bwon pohmehreejoh*
Good evening	Buona sera	*Bwonah sehrah*
Goodnight	Buona notte	*Bwonah nohteh*
My name is ...	Mi chiamo ...	*Mee kyahmoh ...*
NUMBERS		
One	Uno	*Oonoh*
Two	Due	*Dooeh*
Three	Tre	*Treh*
Four	Quattro	*Kwahtroh*
Five	Cinque	*Cheenkweh*
Six	Sei	*Say*
Seven	Sette	*Sehteh*
Eight	Otto	*Ohtoh*
Nine	Nove	*Nohveh*
Ten	Dieci	*Dyehchee*
Twenty	Venti	*Ventee*
Fifty	Cinquanta	*Cheenkwahntah*
One hundred	Cento	*Chentoh*
SIGNS & NOTICES		
Airport	Aeroporto	*Ahehrohpohrtoh*
Railway station	Stazione ferroviaria	*Statsyoneh fehrohveeahreeyah*
Platform	Binario	*Beenahreeyoh*
Smoking/non-smoking	Fumatori/non fumatori	*Foomatohree/non foomahtohree*
Toilets	Bagni	*Bahnyee*
Ladies/Gentlemen	Signore/Signori	*Seenyoreh/Seenyohree*
Subway	Metropolitana	*Mehtrohpohleetahnah*